GOING OUT IN STYLE

...G OUT IN STYLE

THE ARCHITECTURE OF ETERNITY

Douglas Keister

Introduction by Xavier A. Cronin

☑ Facts On File, Inc.

GOING OUT IN STYLE : THE ARCHITECTURE OF ETERNITY

Facts On File, Inc.
11 Penn Plaza
New York NY 10001

Library of Congress Cataloging-in-Publication Data

Keister, Douglas.
Going out in style : the architecture of eternity / Douglas Keister ; introduction by Xavier A. Cronin.
p.   cm.
Includes bibliographical references.
ISBN 0-8160-3649-7
1. Mausoleums—United States—Themes, motives.   I. Title.
NA6150.K45   1997
726´.8´0973—dc21   97-26126

Facts On File books are available at special discounts when purchased in bulk quantities for businesses, associations, institutions or sales promotions. Please call our Special Sales Department in New York at (212) 967-8800 or (800) 322-8755.

The photograph on page 11, from *Architecture and the After-life*, by Howard Montagu Colvin, copyright © 1991 by Yale Univesity Press, is reprinted by permission of the publisher.

You can find Facts On File on the World Wide Web at http://www.factsonfile.com

Text and cover design by Cathy Rincon

Printed in Hong Kong

PAR FOF 10 9 8 7 6 5 4 3 2 1

MILLIONAIRES ROW
Mountain View Cemetery
Oakland, California

(*On previous spread*) The eternal addresses of some of the San Francisco Bay Area's most prominent citizens may be found in Mountain View Cemetery's Millionaires Row. The two lanes that make up Millionaires Row offer spectacular vistas and architectural wonders. The eclecticism of late nineteenth- and early twentieth-century architecture is quite evident here. Among the grand mausoleums, one can find examples of Egyptian Revival, Classical Revival, Romanesque Revival, Gothic Revival, Tholos forms and "uniquely funerary" styles.

Mountain View Cemetery is one of the most attractively sited cemeteries in the United States. Its 220 acres of rolling hills and winding lanes were designed in 1863 by Fredrick Law Olmsted, who also landscaped Central Park, in New York City, and Golden Gate Park, in San Francisco. Olmsted's design for Mountain View emphasizes the harmony between people and the natural features of the landscape.

Garden cemeteries like Mountain View were established in response to the overcrowding of city churchyards and a more optimistic attitude in the culture toward death and the afterlife. These new attitudes and the bucolic settings of garden cemeteries made them an attractive destination for a Victorian family seeking respite from the hustle and bustle of big city life.

Ars longa,

vita brevis

ACKNOWLEDGMENTS

Going Out in Style: The Architecture of Eternity was a collaboration from the outset. I was in the middle of photographing a book, The Bungalow: America's Arts and Crafts Home, with architectural historian Paul Duchscherer. We had a few minutes to spare before we had to be at a house we were to photograph. The house was near Mountain View Cemetery, so we drove over for a look. Paul pointed out the various architectural styles of the mausoleums, and after a few minutes I became enthralled with the idea of photographing these architectural gems.

Eventually I hooked up with Xavier Cronin, an editor at American Cemetery magazine, and in short order, Xavier and I were on a mission to find and document some of America's finest examples of funerary art. Xavier and I wish to thank the cemetery personnel who assisted us on our quest and all of the other folks who helped us.

Thanks to Herb Stansbury and Liz Susman at Mountain View Cemetery; Richard Moylan at Green-Wood Cemetery; Ed Laux and Jeanne Capodilupo at Woodlawn Cemetery; Dan Glavin, Letty Murray and the Historic Oakwood Cemetery Preservation Association; Bill Clendaniel, Janet Heywood, Meg Winslow and the Friends of Mount Auburn Cemetery; Joe Direso, Marie Kalinoski and the Friends of Laurel Hill Cemetery; Tom Earing, Bill Proud and Mike the mausoleum-tender at West Laurel Hill; Fred Whaley and Bette Rupp at Forest Lawn Cemetery; Tom Roberts and Barbara Wirkowski at Allegheny Cemetery; Jack McKinney at Mount Hope Cemetery; Tom Smith and Monica Glatthaar at Spring Grove Cemetery; Derleth Blaine at Cave Hill Cemetery; Aki Lew at Graceland Cemetery; Hughes Drum at Metairie Cemetery; Seraphin Mora, Ken Varner and Kent Seavey at Cypress Lawn Memorial Park; George Nemeth at Lakeview Cemetery; Bob Lefebvre at Olivet Memorial Park; Joe Germaine at Albany Rural Cemetery; Ed Faulkner at Rosehills Cemetery; Marjorie Strong and Karen Lane at the Aldrich Public Library; Tom Burrington and Paul Hutchins at Rock of Ages Granite; Jim McCarthy at Amador Memorial Company; Yvette DeAndreis at The California Historical Society; Nick Verrastro at American Cemetery magazine; Joe Budzinski at Cemetery Management magazine; Debra Richards and Charles Cash at the Louisville Landmarks Commission; Mary Jean Kinshaw at the Filson Club/Louisville; Ted Michel; Laura Schweitzer; Chris Schweitzer; Larry Sloane; John Siegfried; Dale Suess; Doug Boilesen; Norm and Laverne Fisher/Fisher Photo; Karl Grossner/Computer Wizardry; Mark Davis/Net Crawler extraordinaire; Yosh Asato at The American Institute of Architects/San Francisco; Rita Jamison; and Arrol Gellner.

There is a special group of people who championed the idea of this book as soon as they heard about it. It includes my editor at Penguin USA, Cyril I. Nelson, who wanted the book but who knew Facts On File would produce a fabulous edition; our agent Julie Castiglia, who kept the faith and pounded on publishers' doors until she found the right one; Paul Duchscherer, for his knowledge of architecture; John Freed, who suggested the title; Katherine Keister (Mom), who thought it was the best idea I ever had; and Xavier's wife Lucie, who accompanied us to our first cemetery.

The most important acknowledgment goes to my wife, Sandy Schweitzer, who went on photo shoots, researched in libraries, made suggestions, proofread and both encouraged and put up with my obsession with documenting and celebrating some of America's most inspiring architecture.

CONTENTS

PREFACE

I received a call in the spring of 1995 from a photographer named Doug Keister. I was an editor at *American Cemetery* magazine at the time, and Doug, known for his "Painted Ladies" books on Victorian architecture, was working on a new project: a book of America's mausoleums.

The idea came to Doug when strolling through Mountain View Cemetery in Oakland, California, where he lives. He was taken by the sprawling buildings rising from the landscape like miniature castles built by royalty. This was exquisite architecture — Greek temples, Gothic cathedrals, Egyptian pyramids. Beautiful angels flanked bronze doors.

Mountain View is not unique. It is one of dozens of American cemeteries with magnificent mausoleums representing the best of the country's revival architecture, built by wealthy capitalists during the industrial boom of the nineteenth and early twentieth centuries. Had no one captured them in a picture book? The answer was no; Doug had found his next project — one I was eager to participate in.

In August we met at New York's JFK airport and began a week-long journey in my Honda Civic to eleven cemeteries in the Northeast. We began in Brooklyn and proceeded across the Hudson River to Linden, New Jersey, on to Philadelphia, Pittsburgh, Buffalo, Syracuse, Rochester and Albany, New York. Boston's Mount Auburn Cemetery, America's first "rural" cemetery, was a must; we ended our trip back in New York at Woodlawn Cemetery in the Bronx, where we ran out of time trying to shoot a representative sampling of 1,000 mausoleums in a monstrously spectacular display of postmortem architecture

A few months later, Doug flew to Louisville, Kentucky, to photograph Cave Hill Cemetery, and I met him in Cincinnati at the sprawling 750-acre Spring Grove Cemetery. Summer 1996 found us in Chicago, where, in addition to shooting Graceland Cemetery, we unexpectedly came upon the Bohemian National Cemetery and took a few minutes to see what was there. We found just one subject that we knew would be a keeper, and it wasn't even a mausoleum. It was *The Pilgrim*, a bronze Grim Reaper–esque figure on its way to the entrance of a wealthy Czech banker's mausoleum, a fitting back cover for a book on spectacular tombs. The project ended with a grueling shoot of half a dozen cemeteries in New Orleans's oppressive humidity.

Going Out in Style was Doug Keister's brainchild from the beginning, and he is to be commended for persevering when the rejections came fast and unforgivingly. We have felt from the outset that this would be a landmark book, one that needed to be done, and we appreciate those who helped us as we kept the project alive.

We invite you to take a look at America's most unspoiled and fascinating source of historic architecture, mausoleums—the architecture of eternity.

COMMUNITY MAUSOLEUM

Mountain View Cemetery
Oakland, California

(*Opposite*) The 57,000-square-foot community mausoleum in Oakland's Mountain View Cemetery is a 1930s' abstraction of Classical architecture. The colossal scale of the antefixes that cap the colonnades is truly remarkable. The influence of Art Deco style can be seen in the geometry of the capitals, the severe columns with lack of entasis (taper) and smooth walls setting off spare ornamentation. This combination of classical influences on otherwise modern lines is typical of the transitional architecture seen in public buildings of the 1930s.

Mountain View, which was opened in 1865, was one of the last of the true garden cemeteries. Tulip time at Mountain View is an excellent example of the belief of the cemetery's designer, Frederick Law Olmsted, that cemeteries should resemble gardens rather than parks. The 21,000 Darwin-hybrid tulips bloom in eighteen massive beds in the cemetery's gardens.

ARMY OF TENNESSEE TUMULUS

Metairie Cemetery
New Orleans, Louisiana

⟶

Astride his noble steed, Fire Eater, General Albert Sidney Johnston, Confederate States of America, directs his troops to charge the Union lines on the first day of the Battle of Shiloh. Seconds later he was felled by a Yankee bullet, ending his brief but illustrious career. Now he is frozen for all time directing automobiles, trucks and motor homes speeding toward downtown New Orleans on Interstate 10.

The general and his steed crown the 30-foot-high Benevolent Association, Army of Tennessee, Louisiana Division tumulus in Metairie Cemetery. Off to the right and out of view is a life-size statue of a Confederate soldier calling a roll of the honored dead. Entering the tomb through the Gothic archway, one sees forty-eight crypts containing the remains of members of the Society, three of which are sealed for all time by "Action of the Association." These crypts contain the remains of Colonel Charles Didier Dreux, the first Confederate field officer to be killed in battle; General Pierre Gustave Toutant Beauregard, who ordered the first shot fired at Fort Sumter; and John Dimitry, the man who wrote General Johnston's epitaph.

There were many members of the Benevolent Association; consequently, there wasn't room enough in the tumulus for all of them. Once the spaces were filled and another member died, one of the crypts was opened, the remains were scooped up, placed on lead sheets and the sheets were soldered together. The package was then tagged and placed in a large receiving vault in the back. There are no members of the association left alive (the last interment was in 1929), so now the bones of the soldiers of the Army of Tennessee may rest easy.

INTRODUCTION

by Xavier A. Cronin

The ground was not the place for the bodies of America's tycoons of the nineteenth and early twentieth centuries. Theirs would be interior entombment, "aboveground interment," in the parlance of the cemetery business. With money to burn and egos to appease, they decided to leave the world as the powerful of antiquity had: entombed in mausoleums in the great "rural" cemeteries that began appearing outside our cities in the 1830s.

And so America experienced a Golden Age of Mausoleums, ending roughly with the start of the Great Depression. By that time our burial grounds had the look of the "architectural common market" of the Roman Empire under Augustus Caesar, as architecture scholar Howard Colvin puts it, although Gothic, Renaissance and modern influences made them seem more like architectural free-for-alls, with some of the hippest (and strangest) buildings in town. Bankers, industrialists, robber barons, entrepreneurs, adventurers — anyone with the money and ambition to go out in ostentatious style — committed their mortal remains to a showy mausoleum.

Like pharaohs in pyramids and emperors in funerary temples, they would be remembered, if not for their accomplishments, then for their tombs. The eternal abodes of publishing czar William Randolph Hearst, lumber merchant Henry Harrison Getty, coal king Edward J. Berwind, railroad maven Charles Crocker, steamboat captain Harry Spotts and hundreds of others have joined the ranks of humanity's architecture of eternity.

Postmortem Revival

Revival architecture dominates rural cemeteries: Egyptian pyramids; Classical temples; Romanesque fortresses; Gothic cathedrals; Renaissance chapels; Islamic domes. Modern styles also appear here and there, like Sullivanesque cubes, as well as fantastical domes, drums, canopies and other forms, fusing a mix of styles we call "uniquely funerary." Bulging out of the ground at New Orleans cemeteries are "tumuli" mausoleums — burial mounds traced to Neolithic times. Rising above a ravine at Oakwood Cemetery in Syracuse, New York, is a rusticated granite tepee — a "stupa" Buddhist temple reincarnated as the mausoleum of Dr. John M. Wieting, a feisty lecturer likened to Mark Twain, who designed his tomb in 1880 following a trip around the world.

By the end of the nineteenth century, American cemeteries were packed with massive and beautiful buildings fit for the ancients, now fit for rich Americans. This was the Victorian age and maudlin excess and ornamentation was in vogue, in keeping with a cult of mourning that garbed women in black to the tips of their fingers and displayed lockets of the deceased's hair framed on the wall. Funerals were a big deal for the Victorians, as were fashionable mausoleums. Tiffany stained glass windows top altars; fanged gargoyles protrude from eaves; angels and pharaohs grace mausoleum doors as bronze bas-reliefs. The mausoleum itself is often adorned with baroque ornamental tracery and statuary.

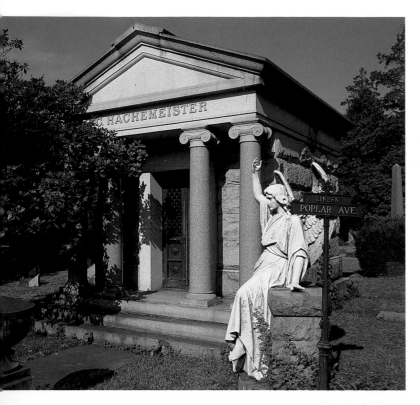

TRAFFIC ANGEL
Woodlawn Cemetery
Bronx, New York

Garden cemeteries, such as Woodlawn in the Bronx, were a departure from the overcrowded and stark churchyards and graveyards that were literally overflowing with bodies and choked with noxious vapors.

Designers of these new garden cemeteries sought to provide a bucolic setting inviting to strollers, carriage riders and picnickers. Where the land was flat, they designed winding roadways to break up the monotony of the landscape and to encourage more leisurely travel. Indeed, in today's world, real estate developers designing tract homes employ the same device to break up the monotony of the barren suburban landscape.

While driving through one of the garden cemeteries with their serpentine roadways, it is easy to get lost. It's always a blessing to find a friendly angel to guide you along the way.

MAUSOLEUM WASHING
West Laurel Hill Cemetery
Bala Cynwyd, Pennsylvania

The cemetery maintenance crew uses a mobile washing system to clean a mausoleum on a hot August day. West Laurel Hill Cemetery was established in response to size limitations imposed by nearby Laurel Hill Cemetery. Laurel Hill was Philadelphia's first rural cemetery and the second rural cemetery established in the United States. In 1867, the city of Philadelphia created a park that effectively enclosed Laurel Hill cemetery and prevented any further expansion. The board of managers of Laurel Hill found an additional 180 acres of land available approximately 1 mile away, where they established West Laurel Hill Cemetery. The first burial at West Laurel Hill was the reinterment of Frederick and Elizabeth Eckert, whose bodies were moved from nearby Mechanics Cemetery.

West Laurel Hill has one of the best collections of well-maintained mausoleums in the country. Through a well-funded program of perpetual care, its mausoleums are cleaned and maintained on a regular basis. The cemetery is thought to contain the costliest collection of marble and granite in Pennsylvania.

The McCan mausoleum at Metairie Cemetery in New Orleans echoes the Albert Memorial in London, which began Queen Victoria's relentless campaign of monument building and the Victorian obsession with funerary architecture. Dominating McCan's mausoleum is an oversized spire rising from an arched square chamber. Flanking steps to an iron door are draped urns in front of mourning figures on pedestals, hands over chests, doleful remorse on their faces. Inside, a stained glass window filters delicate light onto the tomb.

Politically correct mausoleums paid homage to the Christian and pagan worlds. The Van Ness/Parsons mausoleum at Brooklyn's Green-Wood Cemetery is a pyramid with pedimented entrance. Outside, an unlikely (if not blasphemous) scene unfolds: A friendly sphinx looks up adoringly at the Virgin Mary (holding the Christ Child), while Saint Joseph (with lamb cradled in left arm) stands solemnly on a pedestal on the other side of steps leading to a bronze door.

America's rural cemeteries were often advertised as democratic burial grounds, but real estate was real estate and it had a price; those with money bought the choicest plots and proceeded to build spectacular mausoleums and monuments. They spared no expense on this postmortem indulgence. Dropping a hundred thousand dollars or more for an architecturally splendid home for the family's mortal remains was another way to keep up with or surpass one's fellow elite. A walk through a rural cemetery makes it clear that serious competition was at work.

Top architects were hired. James Renwick, whose work includes New York's St. Patrick's Cathedral, has several pieces 10 miles north of the famed cathedral at Woodlawn Cemetery in the Bronx, including the Gothic bronze-domed mausoleum of meatpacker Herman Armour. Chicago's Graceland Cemetery is best known for the cubist perfection of Louis Sullivan's Getty Tomb, believed to be the first "modern" American building (1890) and earning the architect his own Sullivanesque sobriquet. New Orleans's greatest architect, the Frenchman Jacques Nicolas Bussière de Pouilly, designed St. Louis Cathedral and the Royal Orleans Hotel, as well as miniature mausoleums and house tombs in St. Louis Cemetery No. 2. London native Bernard J. S. Cahill, known for inventing the world standard "butterfly map," became resident architect at Cypress Lawn Memorial Park outside San Francisco, designing mausoleums, the administration building and a columbarium (for urns packed with cremated remains). Arthur Page

ZINC TOMBSTONE
Lake View Cemetery
Seattle, Washington

If one preferred ground burial and could not afford a custom-carved tombstone, a host of companies offered molded metal monuments. The metal of choice was usually zinc, which, when subjected to the weather, takes on the blue-gray color of granite.

Purveyors of metal tombstones offered a variety of styles that could be individualized with different combinations of removable panels. These panels could be embossed with hourglasses, floral displays, pithy prose or bucolic scenes — and, of course, the departed's name in a variety of type styles.

In most cases, the metal tombstones wear much better than stone, especially marble, and even after a century of exposure to the elements, continue to resemble recently carved granite.

Brown, designer of the Classical Crocker mausoleum in Mountain View Cemetery, won the California building design competition at the 1893 Chicago Columbian Exposition. John Russell Pope designed the Jefferson Memorial in Washington, as well as five Woodlawn mausoleums, including the Egyptian Revival temple mausoleum of department store magnate F. W. Woolworth.

Artistic Representations

Reproduced in rural cemeteries are artistic representations of the great buildings of antiquity — including the Pantheon, Parthenon and Tower of the Winds — and of the Renaissance. A full-scale replica of Leonardo da Vinci's tomb, the huge and heavily gargoyled fifteenth-century St. Hubert Chapel, was built from Indiana limestone in 1903 and stands among Woodlawn's awesome display of some 1,000 mausoleums. The open-air French Temple of Love tholos tomb in Louisville's Cave Hill Cemetery was commissioned by socialite Dr. Preston

FAMILY TOMB
Greenwood Cemetery
New Orleans, Louisiana

The concept of prefabricated homes was popularized during the Victorian era. Prospective homeowners could scan Sears, Roebuck, Montgomery Ward and a host of other catalogs to order the home of their dreams — precut and delivered to their building site. For a few dollars more, the catalog company would also send a crew to assemble the house.

Along the same line, families who could not afford a custom-made or architect-designed mausoleum could buy a prefabricated one and have it delivered and assembled on-site. The Milten Berger Company of New Orleans offered its cast-iron tomb to less affluent folks who desired aboveground burial. The tomb provided a space above the entry for the name of the occupant — in this case, I. N. Marks. to make sure no one mistook the tomb for a storage shed, the manufacturer clearly labeled each of its creations "Family Tomb."

Pope Satterwhite for his wife. John Russell Pope's mausoleum for stockbroker Jules Bache is a full-scale replica of the Egyptian Kiosk of Trajan. A lesser-known replica stands at Metairie Cemetery — the "ruined castle" Egan mausoleum, a deceptively tattered open-air structure of Tennessee marble with a triumphal arch fronting a rectangular facade (and two uneven towers shoring up the rear), modeled after the ruins of a chapel on Egan's estate in County Cork, Ireland. Rising 70 feet from a summit at Syracuse's Oakwood Cemetery is the Cornelius Tyler Longstreet pyramid mausoleum, a near double of Rome's Caius Cestius mausoleum (first century B.C.), down to shrubs sprouting from the joints of the stone blocks (although Longstreet's sealed stone door is besmirched with graffiti, and wood and ash from spent campfires often litter its base).

Granite Influence

Most mausoleums of this era are made of granite, marble and various types of stone, although some settled for concrete, cast iron and other more affordable materials. The granite quarry industry came into its own in the nineteenth century, and the cemetery was one more place where granite structures were reared. Granite had became a favorite material for mausoleums "by reason of its stain-resistance, uniform texture, and susceptibility to high polish . . ." according to a history of the granite industry in Barre, Vermont. Monument companies were the frontline operators, bidding on projects and hiring artists, craftsmen and granite haulers. New Orleans monument maven Albert Weiblen leased a quarry at Stone Mountain, Georgia, and from the 1890s through the first half of the twentieth century his firm produced many pieces in Metairie Cemetery, which ranks with Woodlawn as the country's mausoleum showcase.

Often massive granite slabs had to be delivered from the quarry to the sheds where carvers practiced their craft. The legendary Fayette "Fay" Cutler, a quarry crew boss, is known for his Herculean feat in 1888 of harnessing 40 horses to drag two 50-ton granite slabs down 4 miles of hill in Barre for a Classical Revival mausoleum to be erected 3,000 miles away at Stanford University in Northern California. It took Cutler and horses eighteen days to get the first slab down, but a snowstorm provided a nice base for the second, which made it down much faster. The slabs were dragged to the carvers' shed, and when the pieces were ready, they were again dragged to the rail station — the Vermont Central Railroad had recently gone on-line — and shipped to Palo Alto via Los Angeles.

Fay apparently was looking for bigger slabs, or perhaps he was just in great demand. Soon after his 50-ton job he took on a 175-ton pink granite boulder, which he moved 9 miles to the mausoleum of industrialist John Crouse at Syracuse's Oakwood Cemetery.

Some were not so demanding of their tombs, opting for "cookie-cutter" models that could have come from the pages of a Sears, Roebuck catalog for pre-assembled homes. Introduced to New Orleans cemeteries were cloned family tomb pillboxes, tinny affairs cordoned off with wrought-iron fence, hardly worthy of the term mausoleum. Not everyone was inclined (or financially able) to construct grandiose buildings to contain the family's remains. In many cemeteries, the simple Greek temple became the standard, elegant and neat, but overwhelmed by the elaborate structures around them.

Lunar Landers

The imagination of the architect (or client) working on a mausoleum sometimes ran wild. These "uniquely funerary" buildings were born of a fusion of styles and uncategorizable elements. You won't see buildings like this elsewhere, and they give cemeteries a trace of the fantasy park. Touching down at Chicago's Graceland Cemetery is what looks like a medieval lunar landing vehicle — a dome that wants to be a triangle sprouting off a square base formed with high triumphal arches (the Huck family mausoleum). The sandstone Moorhead mausoleum in Pittsburgh's Allegheny Cemetery sprouts delicate green plants from a giant musty brown dome — an octagon also ready for a distant moon landing. (Padlocks on Moorhead's door must be replaced every few years following break-ins by ghoulish partyers.)

A humongous granite ball, shiny, glistening and ridiculously oversized, tops the domed cookie-jar Kampfe mausoleum at Brooklyn's Green-Wood Cemetery in a charmingly absurd fit. The Bigelow Chapel at Boston's Mount Auburn Cemetery looks like a cross between the palace of the Wizard of Oz and the animated castle at the beginning of the 1960s Walt Disney television show, with finial-topped spires rising 100 feet from all sides. Green-Wood's wildly decorated catafalque canopy tomb of John Matthews, the "Soda Fountain King," is best described by author Peter

FAY CUTLER, GRANITE MOVER
Barre, Vermont

It was Fay Cutler's job to move two 50-ton slabs of granite (the largest ever moved), down the hill from the quarry in Graniteville to the stone sheds in Barre. From there, the finished gable stones were to be placed on railroad cars bound for California for use in constructing the Stanford mausoleum in Palo Alto.

Cutler devised a system using rollers and horses (six horses in front to guide it and thirty-four horses behind, to keep it from going too fast) to inch the slabs down the hill. The first slab's journey took eighteen and a half days and was closely followed by the local paper. Luckily a snowstorm moved into the area in time to move the second slab. Cutler was able to use sleds on the snow instead of rollers, considerably reducing the time needed to move the second slab to the stone sheds.

GABLE STONES
Stanford Mausoleum
Barre, Vermont

The finished gable stones for the Stanford mausoleum outside a stone shed in Barre, Vermont, circa 1888.

STANFORD MAUSOLEUM
Stanford University Campus
Palo Alto, California

After its 3,000-mile journey, the Stanford mausoleum was assembled in a secluded glen on the campus of Stanford University in Palo Alto, California. The finished product is a Classical Revival temple with sphinxes ready to guard the Stanford remains.

ITALIAN STONE CARVERS
Barre, Vermont

Most of the work of cutting and carving granite in Vermont was done by Scottish and Italian immigrants. The most delicate carving was generally carried out by the Italians. As children, the Italians had worked in the stone sheds in their native Milan. They went to school at night to be carvers, and if they had skill and good luck, by age twenty-five or thirty they might be allowed to carve on their own. Many moved to Vermont and found work in the quarries and stone sheds of Vermont.

Even in the heyday of mausoleum construction, from 1880 to 1920, there were only a few dozen carvers doing the most intricate work.

The January 9, 1926, edition of the *Boston Evening Transcript* presaged the end of the grand mausoleums, reporting, "There are but five carvers now, and only one man to move their statues over the country and never chip a corner. But will there ever be another Fayette Cutler, who will move anything under the sun, or another Tozi, or Mori, or Sanguinetti, or Corti, or Melnati? . . . A little known race of artists is passing; there are none to take their place."

MATT HALEY, MAUSOLEUM SETTER

Nowadays, many smaller family mausoleums are delivered to cemetery sites fully assembled. During the Golden Age of the Mausoleum, when structures were considerably larger and more complex than they are today, they were assembled on-site by specialized crews trained in mausoleum erection. This photograph appeared in an advertisement offering the skills of "Matt Haley, Monument and Mausoleum Setter."

Hellman: "Toothsome gargoyles guard its four corners, while squirrels, lizards, frogs, rats, bears, wolves and lions seem to scurry, crawl or stalk over the ultra-ornate Neo-Gothic superstructure of the tomb. Amid four granite pillars rests Matthews's sarcophagus. His likeness stares up at scenes from his life, including his youthful farewell to his mother as he boards a ship for America and his contemplation of the fizzy invention that would make him rich."[1]

What's Inside

The dead, of course, in their caskets, loaded into crypts, usually set in floors, side walls or serving as altars below a stained glass window. Viewing the mausoleums from the outside, it's easy to forget they are more than architecture, that they are first and foremost tombs.

Some have dozens of crypts, enough for several generations of the family clan. Woodlawn's Ehret mausoleum, a Romanesque Revival fortress complete with lions guarding the entrance, boasts fifty-six crypts, twenty-eight in each sidewall. More than a few crypts are empty, and may be forever, as is the case with many mausoleums. Families have scattered to distant locations so that sometimes what was once planned as the tomb for generations to come, the family mausoleum, has been abandoned, forgotten or relegated to a curious, macabre relic.

Ghost stories abound. One comes from Mike, a mausoleum-tender at Philadelphia's West Laurel Hill, who grew up nearby. When Mike was a kid the story went that a ghost lived in the George Miller "Keep" mausoleum — a rock-solid minicastle we were unable to get into after half an hour of jiggling keys that seemed to fit but would not open the heavy iron-work door. "When I'd walk up through the cemetery during closing hours," Mike remembers, "I used to be scared of this, because they told me a witch lived in there. I was always frightened, I wouldn't go near it: 'Don't go up there,' they'd say. 'A witch lives up in there!'" (Perhaps that's why the original owner sold it to George Miller.)

Although we couldn't finagle our way into the Miller mausoleum, we were able to enter others. What we found ranged from tidy chapels with urns on a sarcophagus serving as an altar (plus utility closets for brooms and picker-uppers), to dark, musty rooms with concrete floors, unvisited for years if not decades, with half the crypts empty—fitting material for Poe or Stephen King. The last entombment at Mount Auburn Cemetery's Bourne mausoleum was in 1889; facing you as you enter this Romanesque bunker is the bust of a man against the back wall bathed in daylight under a domed skylight. The bust does not identify the man (Bourne himself?); it only states that it was sculpted in Italy. Two rows of white marble crypts line the sidewalls, with a rusty paste of ooze crusting one. Mount Auburn hasn't heard from the family in years.

Here's a description of the inside of the Lewis Henry Morgan mausoleum in Mount Hope Cemetery in Rochester, New York, as told by Mount Hope's veteran tour guide, Jack McKinney, during a private showing for us: "The inside is just a plain unfinished brick wall, with the mortar still dripping. No bricks on the sides, they're all on the wall facing the door as you go in. Into that wall [are] the ends of the coffins. Instead of having slabs over the grave, you have a slab in the wall [sealing the crypt] that carries the inscriptions. About twelve [crypts] are available, only seven or eight have been used."

A spiral staircase (inspected once a year by Mike the mausoleum-tender) takes you to the wall and floor crypts in the copper-domed Betz mausoleum at West Laurel Hill. Two white-marble crypts serve as an altar inside Woodlawn's John F. Martin Byzantine Revival chapel mausoleum, where mosaic murals decorate arched walls and a stained glass window behind the altar shows Christ, flanked by angels, ascending to heaven.

From Tumulus to Mausoleum

Elaborate tombs for the dead have been around for thousands of years. The pyramids are the largest and most famous, but nomadic Neolithic man also entombed chieftains and other revered leaders thousands of years ago in subterranean and aboveground structures in Europe and the western Mediterranean. Like the pyramids, hundreds if not thousands of men toiled for months or years to build them.

The Neolithics' tomb of choice was the tumulus — a circular mound dug out of the earth that opened into a central domed chamber. From the chambers, passageways led to tombs or tomb pits. Hundreds of Neolithic tombs survive in the British Isles and Ireland, including open-field huts made of gigantic stone slabs weighing as much as the slabs Fay Cutler and his horses hauled down

STONEHENGE MEMORIAL
Maryhill, Washington

This cenotaph (a monument built to a person or persons whose remains lie elsewhere) was erected by noted eccentric Sam Hill, whose own tomb lies a mere 50 yards away, to commemorate thirteen young Klickitat County men who gave their lives in World War I. The altar stone was dedicated on July 4, 1918, and the full structure was completed and dedicated on May 30, 1929. Sam Hill had the structure fabricated out of concrete to resemble how the original megalithic Stonehenge on Salisbury Plain in Wiltshire, England must have appeared c. 1350 B.C. Sam Hill's Stonehenge sits high on a bluff overlooking the Columbia River near Maryhill, Washington.

During a total eclipse of the sun in February 1979, Stonehenge, not surprisingly, became a center of activity. Thousands of people, including members of the New Order of Reformed Druids, gathered at Sam Hill's concrete creation to witness the moon "eating the sun." Participants sang and chanted in the darkness until the sun again emerged from behind the moon.

Sam Hill also built a town (Maryhill) and a museum (the Maryhill Museum), both named for his wife, Mary, on his isolated property. He was noted for his eccentric ways and has achieved a measure of immortality in the oft-used phrase, "What the Sam Hill are you doing?"

THE MAUSOLEUM OF HALICARNASSUS

This is a conjectural reconstruction of the monument in accordance with modern scholarship. Only the major elements of the sculptural decoration are indicated.

the hills of Barre for nineteenth-century American mausoleum builders.

The tumulus endured over millennia even as aboveground tombs dethroned it as the predominant burial structure. Change was gradual, and the ancients built tumuli even as temples and domed tombs arose in the early centuries B.C. Tumuli inspired the nineteenth-century mausoleum-in-a-hillside, which was fused into the land; genuine tumuli can be found here and there in American cemeteries. New Orleans has a few notable examples, including Metairie Cemetery's Army of Tennessee and Louisiana Civil War monument-mausoleum, a green mushroomlike mound topped by a soldier on horseback pointing with binoculars toward the flow of traffic on the highway 50 feet behind him. A quarter of a mile away in Greenwood Cemetery is another well-manicured tumulus mound with an elk topping a Classical Greek facade — the communal mausoleum of the Benevolent and Protective Order of Elks, No. 30 — (a clock atop the building is stopped at 11 o'clock, and there's a bit of a tilt to the structure from an unstable foundation).

In time the subterranean tumulus was supplanted by aboveground structures of marked architecture, reflecting changing attitudes toward what tombs are. Among Neolithic peoples, the dead were thought to be engaged in a long, deep slumber and were to be protected until they awoke. The ancients were more interested in flaunting the status of the entombed and sought to provide fitting structures to honor them. Warriors and statesmen and various esteemed persons were often accorded semidivine status. The first temple-tombs were often considered *heroons*, the tombs of heros. Whatever one believed with regard to the afterlife, the need to honor dead heros and rulers was unquestioned. As architectural scholar Howard Colvin puts it: "Once great men were accorded divine honours, then it followed that their tombs should be conceived in the likeness of the temples of the gods." [2]

King Mausolus

The word *mausoleum* is derived from the name Mausolus, king of Halicarnassus, a great harbor city in the kingdom of Caria in Asia Minor (modern Turkey), whose tomb was a huge fortress built in 353 B.C. by Mausolus's wife Artemisia (who happened also to be his sister). When Mausolus died, grief-stricken Artemisia

decided a fitting tribute to him would be a vast and elaborately decorated tomb. (Some accounts show construction began while the king was still alive.) Inspiration for what would become the world's first mausoleum is believed to have come from the Nereid tomb, a temple on a podium converted into a tomb for a Lycian (Greek) chieftain about 400 B.C. Friezes on the Nereid tomb depict battles between the Greeks and Amazons, with whimsical female statues standing between Ionic columns.

The tomb at Halicarnassus, much larger than the Nereid but emulating its decorative and narrative style, emerged as a rectangular fortress five stories high with hundreds of statues decorating all quarters. It was "surrounded by a colonnade of 36 columns," writes Colvin "[supporting] a pyramidal superstructure receding in 24 steps to the summit. On the top was a four-horse chariot of marble . . . By fusing tall podium, temple columns and pyramidal roof into one, the designers of the Mausoleum had created a new architectural formula for the glorification of the dead." [3]

The dome was not to be outdone by the temple and pyramid. About the same time the Halicarnassus Mausoleum was built, giant domed tombs on podiums appeared in North Africa, and the dome evolved into the tomb of choice for many in the ancient, medieval and modern world.

Alas, nothing is left of Mausolus's tomb except parts of its foundation. It was probably damaged in a thirteenth-century earthquake and destroyed by the Knights of St. John of Jerusalem, who plundered the structure at the end of the fifteenth and the early sixteenth centuries and made off with the stones to strengthen one of their castles. In addition, the knights destroyed the underground tomb chambers and burned the mausoleum's marble for lime.

It didn't take long for word to spread through the ancient world that Halicarnassus housed a spectacular new building rising majestically above the harbor. Voyagers sailing into the Halicarnassus harbor had never seen anything like Mausolus's tomb, and it was acknowledged as one of the Seven Wonders of the Ancient World. But the city's independence was to be short-lived; about twenty years after the mausoleum was completed, Alexander the Great conquered Halicarnassus. The Greeks adopted the tomb of Mausolus as the new standard and began building their own *mausoleion*, as they called them, coining a term that survives today. The Romans emulated the Greeks and the mausoleum evolved into a staple of the architecture of antiquity in three basic forms — pyramid, dome and rectangular temple with columns, although "uniquely funerary" and modern styles evolved in the Western world in the nineteenth and twentieth centuries.

Onward Christian Martyriums

The mausoleum remained the burial space of choice for the rich and powerful until the rise of Christianity. This came about A.D. 400 with the collapse of the Roman Empire. The Christians had certainly paid their dues: During the first three centuries A.D., many who kept the faith suffered brutal deaths at the hands of Roman persecutors. These martyrs, many of whom became saints, were buried in the Catacombs — underground necropoli, or burial grounds — laid out along the roads to Rome.

The persecutions ended in the early fourth century; 100 years later Christianity was well on its way to becoming the dominant religious and cultural influence in the Western world. Roman Catholic leaders rejected the concept of the mausoleum as a separate tomb building, but they began re-interring martyrs in buildings that became known as martyriums — a place where the faithful could be near those who were thought to have already passed through the Pearly Gates. In keeping with the idea that the body itself would be resurrected (or cast into hell), dead bodies assumed profound significance for Christians. The Romans had kept the dead — no matter how great the personage — out of sight. Some were cremated and their cremated remains stored in decorative urns placed in niched compartments in columbarium rooms. Christians, on the contrary, showcased tombs in ground-level buildings so worshippers could get as close as possible. Relics of the saints, shards of bone and shreds of flesh, for instance, were sought after by those strategizing for a place in heaven. As for cremation, Christians condemned it, for resurrection depended on a *body* planted in the ground (even if it would likely be dust by Judgment Day). Christian persecutors had tormented the Christians on this point by burning some of their martyrs and scattering their cremated remains to the winds as an insult to the Christian God who promised to resurrect them. As you'd expect, this hardened Christians against cremation.

The Catholic church made a good business collecting interment fees and assigning everyone his or her eternal resting place. The important dead were to be buried in the church proper: The martyriums had become shrines (many were built to designs similar to mausoleums) and were later converted into churches. And so churches, chapels and cathedrals were filled with ornate tombs of saints, bishops and priests (the closer to the altar, some believed, the better the odds of a quick entry through heaven's door). Lesser subjects ended up in burial grounds outside town or, space permitting, in churchyard burial grounds. The mausoleum had fallen from grace, as it were, except in the pagan North, where heathens kept entombing their dead as they pleased.

Return of the Mausoleum

It took nearly a thousand years for the mausoleum's return. The Renaissance and Reformation had set the stage. Renaissance artists and architects celebrated the individual, not a deity, and private tombs in the form of mausoleums began appearing here and there. The Reformation spawned Protestant sects that rejected the Catholic belief that souls could be inched toward heaven by prayers and strategic church burial sites. "But to be buried in a mausoleum that stood on its own without any provision for regular religious services was more than a gesture of aristocratic privilege or of neoclassical taste," writes Colvin. "It implied a new attitude towards the afterlife which was at variance with a thousand years of Catholic belief and practice."[4]

It wasn't until the eighteenth century, the century of the Enlightenment, that the mausoleum regained its glory of antiquity. A few major factors contributed to this revival. One was India. As Europeans raided India in the seventeenth and eighteenth centuries, they were fascinated by the beautiful mausoleums they found. Many architects regarded India's magnificent Taj Mahal palace-garden mausoleum, finished in 1630, as the world's most spectacular building. And so Europeans built mausoleums in the grand dome and temple tradition in the cemeteries they laid out in India, and word spread back home.

The eighteenth and nineteenth centuries also saw great archaeological discoveries of ancient ruins. Especially revealing finds were made at Herculaneum and Pompeii, in southern Italy, in 1737 and 1748, respectively. These and other discoveries inspired an Italian architect–illustrator, Giovanni Battista Piranesi, to create hundreds of illustrations and etchings of the architecture of antiquity, including Roman tombs and mausoleums, such as the Tomb of Cecilia Metella, a circular stone castle-like structure. Architects took notice and applied this new source of inspiration to the mausoleums they were designing for wealthy clients.

Protestants in Scotland, England and Sweden had been thinking about reintroducing the mausoleum as early as the seventeenth century, seeing no reason why the dead should be buried in churches. In 1691, Sir George MacKenzie erected a magnificent octagonal mausoleum in Edinburgh; in 1736, another domed mausoleum, this one huge, with a dome set atop a towering Ionic colonnade on a pedestal, was erected at Castle Howard in Yorkshire, England. Soon mausoleums were springing up throughout England, Scotland and Ireland, and by the late eighteenth century, in Germany and Sweden.

Napoleon's incursions into Africa awakened interest in Egyptian architecture, and by the early nineteenth century the architecture of the ancient world had been rediscovered and would soon appear in America's elite burial grounds.

America's Contribution: The Rural Cemetery

The rise of the American mausoleum begins with our first "rural" cemetery — Mount Auburn, just down the street from Harvard Square in Cambridge, Massachusetts.

Mount Auburn opened in 1831. Boston and other American cities had been searching for a solution to the disturbing problem of gnarled and jam-packed churchyards and city graveyards. France had the same problem and dealt with it in the 1790s by opening "garden" cemeteries outside the cities. This was the period of the French Revolution; monarchies were crumbling, democracy was rising, and some were adopting a more romantic view of life and death that embraced the charms of nature and rejected the gloom and doom, fire and brimstone preached through the centuries by the Roman Catholic church. This enlightened attitude spurred some of the French to bury their dead in private gardens, an idea inspired at least in part by British aristocrats who had been erecting funerary monuments in garden estates since the early 1700s. French philosopher Jean-Jacques Rousseau was buried in a garden estate in

1778, and some say the garden burials of Rousseau and other notable Frenchmen were pivotal events in the garden cemetery movement.

On a more pressing level, France's new green-and-clean burial grounds were less a postmortem indulgence than a necessity: Paris's graveyards and "charnel houses" — pits and chambers with graveyard bones — were crammed with the remains of millions. The issue seems to have been forced in 1780 when a few thousand bodies from Cimetière des Innocents (Cemetery of the Holy Innocents), a 1,000-year-old graveyard taking dead bodies from just about anybody who sent them there, crashed through the basement walls of an adjacent apartment building. Needless to say, this fetid mess of human remains reeked, and at least a few apartment dwellers became physically ill as a result. Parisians were not amused by the collapse of their biggest cemetery; a search got on to find a suitable place for the dead.

And so French garden burial grounds, called *champs de repos* (fields of rest) or *lieux de repos* (places of rest) and other euphemisms, were laid out in the late eighteenth century, culminating with Père Lachaise, opening in 1804 (under decree by Napoleon) in a sprawling garden estate occupying a hill overlooking Paris.

Père Lachaise

Père Lachaise was an event, a marriage of the Enlightenment's optimism and the English "picturesque landscape garden" with Neoclassical architecture. The result is a beautiful park that remains one of the world's great burial grounds. Everything smelled rosy at Père Lachaise, bucolic and garden fresh. Lime trees traced narrow roads packed with temple mausoleums leading to the summit. A spirit of one-upsmanship emerged, architects designing what they hoped would be the grandest of mausoleums. The remains of Molière, Beaumarchais and other great Frenchmen were exhumed and reinterred here. By 1830 Père Lachaise had become a tourist attraction (a contemporary favorite attraction is the tomb of American rock star Jim Morrison). More importantly, Père Lachaise had set the standard for solving the burial crowding problem, and by the 1830s the English and Americans had followed its example with their own out-of-city burial grounds.

America's Burial Crunch

By the late eighteenth century, America's city burial grounds were overcrowded; some even reeked with the stench of decomposing bodies in shallow graves. A common sight were tilted and toppled tombstones zigzagging chaotically in wild grass and weeds. The only citizens for whom graveyards were not eyesores were farmers burying their dead on the farm, where there was plenty of space; those out on western trails exploring the wild frontier; and Native Americans, who tended to their dead in coveted sacred burial grounds. Underground church vaults were filling up. Soon the problem would grow worse. The country had just won independence and a burgeoning population crowded the cities: A place would have to be found for tomorrow's dead.

Another concern: People believed corpses emitted fumes, the kind believed to have poisoned those living next to the Paris cemetery that collapsed. Sometimes a

VIEW FROM THE TOMB
St. Louis Cemetery No. 2
New Orleans, Louisiana

The house-tombs of St. Louis Cemetery No. 2 stand in silence as traffic on Interstate 10 whizzes past. St. Louis No. 2 was established in 1823 as a response to the overcrowding of St. Louis Cemetery No. 1. City fathers, ever fearful of noxious vapors emanating from cemeteries, were determined to place St. Louis No. 2 at least 2,400 feet from the city limits; in actuality St. Louis No. 2 was only 1,800 feet from the city limits. Today, the cemetery is completely surrounded by urban sprawl.

Although many of the tombs appear to be quite similar, there are a number of society tombs and private tombs in St. Louis No. 2 that were specially designed. Architect J. N. B. DePouilly, for example, designed many of the tombs at St. Louis No. 2. He came to New Orleans from France in the 1830s with a sketch book filled with scale drawings of some of the finest tombs at Père Lachaise Cemetery in Paris. His designs may be seen throughout New Orleans's many cemeteries.

WALL VAULTS

St. Louis Cemetery No. 1
New Orleans, Louisiana

Although folklore suggests that early New Orleaneans preferred aboveground burial because of the high water table, it is more likely they were emulating their cousins in Europe, where burial above ground was fashionable. In fact, however, in New Orleans's first formal cemetery, the St. Peter Street Cemetery, in what is now the French Quarter, all burials were in the ground.

When St. Louis Cemetery No. 1 was consecrated in 1789, Esteban Miro was the fifth Spanish governor of Louisiana. It is likely that the concept of wall vaults — popular in Seville and other Spanish towns of the time — was adopted by the designers of St. Louis No. 1. Thus, even the less well-to-do, who could not afford a mausoleum, could still be buried fashionably above ground.

Wall vaults, also known as side vaults and oven vaults, served a dual purpose: In addition to providing a last resting place, they were constructed around the perimeter of cemeteries to form a boundary wall. As can be seen in the photograph, they are still in use today.

nasty virus or fever making the rounds of a neighborhood was blamed on the nearby graveyard. Bloated graveyards in New York and New Haven were blamed for yellow fever; church graveyards in Cincinnati were blamed for cholera outbreaks in the 1830s and 1840s, spurring the creation in 1845 of Spring Grove Cemetery.

What to do with the dead? Cremation would have seemed the logical solution, but was rarely practiced and

would not come up for serious discussion until the 1860s; the cremation furnace would not be introduced in America until 1876. Since few people in America adhered to the funerary rituals of India and other countries with Buddhist and Hindu populations, and since the Catholic church forbade cremation, the idea of burning bodies on funeral pyres was not a serious option. So the answer seemed obvious: The dead would have to get out of town. Not too far away — maybe 5

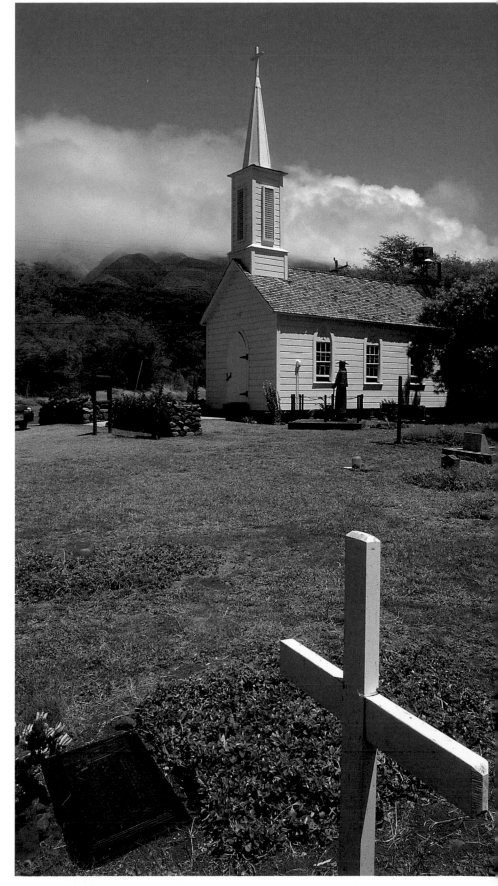

ST. JOSEPH'S CHURCH
Molokai, Hawaii

Prior to the establishment of landscaped garden cemeteries, most people were buried in small family cemeteries or churchyards. The burial grounds around churches were known as "God's acre."

This picturesque church on the island of Molokai in Hawaii was built in 1876 by Father Damien, who is memorialized with a life-size bronze statue outside the church. Father Damien has achieved immortality as the untiring Catholic priest who ministered to the lepers banished to a remote peninsula on Molokai. He lived in the leper colony and ceaselessly championed the lepers' cause, eventually contracting leprosy and dying of the disease. Today, leprosy is fully treatable; leper colonies are, fortunately, a thing of the past.

or 10 miles from city center — but the days of city burials were numbered.

With Père Lachaise making international headlines, Americans discussed the idea of burial grounds outside cities. Boston's mayor set up a commission in 1823 to find such a place; not much happened for a few years, as the people assigned the task were apparently busy with more pressing matters. But a few forward-thinking Bostonians had noted Père Lachaise with great interest.

In the forefront was renaissance man Dr. Jacob Bigelow, a professor at Harvard Medical College and a founder of the Massachusetts Institute of Technology and Massachusetts Horticultural Society. Bigelow, who

CIVIL WAR PLOT
Mount Hope Cemetery
Rochester, New York

Many of the 5,000 men from Rochester who fought in the Civil War are buried in this plot. The plaque on the monument is inscribed:

> By fame's eternal camping ground
> Their silent tents are spread
> And glory guards with solemn round
> The bivouac of the dead.

also dabbled in architecture, engraving and landscape design, finally took the lead in 1831. He and his partners at the Horticultural Society bought 72 acres of woodland, 4 miles outside the city near Harvard College, after securing $60 each from 100 investors who would each acquire a 300-square-foot burial plot. Harvard students had named this peaceful tract — where Emerson, among other notable Harvardites, wandered for inspiration — "Sweet Auburn," after the bucolic village of the same name in the Oliver Goldsmith poem "The Deserted Village" (1770). Bigelow and friends kept "Auburn" but balked at "Sweet" — as beautiful as the place would be, "Sweet Auburn Cemetery" would have been pushing it. Due to a summit on the tract, "Sweet" became "Mount," and America's first cemetery was consecrated on September 24, 1831, amid lofty transcendental sentiments.

Opening ceremonies were held in a cemetery amphitheater. Musicians performed, worshippers sang and Associate Supreme Court Justice Joseph Story delivered the consecration address, during which he pointed out: "Below us flows the winding Charles [River] . . . like the stream of time hastening to the ocean of eternity."

It was an unexpectedly enchanted place, this new burial ground, as Mary Tyler Peabody, an early visitor, discovered. In a letter to a friend, she wrote:

> I thought it was a little hill skirted with wood and water but it is covered with the most luxuriant and varied woodland — paths are cut through it in every direction, and the monuments rise from . . . trees in every direction, enclosed only by a little iron railing . . . and some with flowers. If you follow the windings of the paths you come unexpectedly upon these simple and beautiful obelisks . . . Since they have begun to ornament this beautiful spot, they have opened views of the surrounding country in every direction, which is said to add immeasurably to the beauty of it. One portion of the hill is covered with pines where it is perfectly dark, and the song of those pine trees has been sounding in my ears ever since. We sat down upon all the seats and stumps and staid three hours . . . We at last tore ourselves away from the place, loaded with wild flowers . . . [5]

Writing in 1838, author Enoch Cobb Wines noticed, "Swelling hills, rounded knolls, deep ravines, secluded dells, opening glades, steep acclivities, primeval forest, tiny lakes, and even a quite lofty mountain . . . We spent more than an hour threading these mazy walks, and rambling over this endlessly diversified and most romantic of burial-places; and every turn revealed to our view, and equally to our admiration, some new glory of art in the shape of an obelisk, a column, a sarcophagus . . . each vying with the others in the purity of the taste with which it was designed, and in perfect elegance and finish of its workmanship . . ." [6]

To the modern American, this may seem ovelry sentimental, but Boston was the center of the New England Transcendentalists; nature and art tastefully wedded in a burial ground was big news. Mount Auburn would also honor the memory of patriots: Remains of Revolutionary War heroes were reburied here to receive what they never had in their previous miserable graveyards: monuments erected in their honor and the reverence of thousands of visitors.

Precursor of Public Parks

With the arrival of Mount Auburn, the horror of the graveyard, with its sloppy burials and toppled tombstones, was to be replaced with beautiful parks for the dead. In these beautiful cemeteries, you might forget you walked on consecrated land above dead bodies. These were not graveyards, not burial grounds, but cemeteries," from the Greek word *koiman*, a sleeping chamber. The whole family would sleep together forever, like the family at Mount Auburn, under matching slate tombstones, marked "mother," "father," "son," "daughter," in a secluded enclave shaded by evergreens.

Mount Auburn made news that spread quickly. Soon other major eastern cities rushed to lay out their own cemeteries. In 1835 came Laurel Hill in Philadelphia; in 1838, Green-Wood in Brooklyn and Mount Hope in Rochester; in 1839, Green Mount in Baltimore; in 1841, Albany (N.Y.) Rural Cemetery. Soon rural cemeteries were popping up all over; San Francisco put the West Coast on the burial map in 1854, when Lone Mountain Cemetery opened, boasting a 500-foot summit.

These cemeteries were so beautiful they became a major source of inspiration for the "City Beautiful" movement and our subsequent public parks. Green-Wood in Brooklyn, laid out on farmland overlooking Gowanus Bay, spurred a design competition for New York's Central Park, won by America's great landscape architect, Frederick Law Olmsted, who went on to design Mountain View Cemetery in Oakland.

Among the charms of the rural cemeteries were magnificent views: New York Harbor (and today, the World Trade Center and midtown Manhattan) from a summit at Green-Wood, 220 feet above sea level; a shimmer of Boston's Charles River from Mount Auburn; pretty green meadows at Cincinnati's Spring Grove Cemetery. David Colton chose his mausoleum site at Mountain View in Oakland so his widow could see it from her Nob Hill apartment across the bay in San Francisco.

Rural cemeteries became the place to be buried and a place for the living to get away from the city for a little relaxation and meditation. In the early years of Mount Auburn, this didn't always sit well with plot-owners, who complained about visitors trampling over their burial estates, on foot and in carriages. Most visitors behaved themselves — women strolled under parasols, horse-drawn carriages moved at a trickle's pace, worshippers gathered for Sunday services. But the irreverent scrawled graffiti on trees, slobs left behind picnic debris and chatterboxes spoiled the peace and quiet. Grave robbers sometimes prowled about.

Mount Auburn's founders, now members of the board of directors, were in a quandary: The press condemned them as elitist when they announced the cemetery would be off-limits to anyone but plot-owners, and plot-owners chastised them for allowing their property and privacy to be trampled upon.

A compromise was reached. On Sundays and holidays the cemetery was closed to all but plot-owners, and everyone who entered during regular hours had to buy a ticket and give it to a gatekeeper.

By 1839 Mount Auburn had a set of rules and a 250-page guidebook: The cemetery opened at sunrise, closed at sunset; there would be no shooting off guns, no picking wildflowers, no driving your horse and buggy faster than the flow of pedestrians — and, of course, no body-snatching.

Victorian Death Values

The arrival of survivor-friendly burial grounds paralleled the arrival of sentimental and hopeful attitudes toward death — part of the romanticism and transcendentalism spawned by the Enlightenment. The consecration hymn at Spring Grove's opening in 1845 proclaimed:

Why should the memories of the dead
be ever those of gloom and sadness?
Why should their dwellings not be made
'Mid scenes of light, and life, and gladness?
Here let the young and the gay repair.
And in this scene of light and beauty,
gather from Earth, and Sky and Air,
lessons of Life, and Love and Duty! [7]

Not everyone was so cheery. During Spring Grove's dedication, one John M'Lean reminded his audience of the cold, hard truth of a cold, lifeless body, be it under a spreading chestnut or in a grisly graveyard:

Nature within it may wear a cheerful aspect, and the songsters of the wood may be heard; but the memorials of the grave will be present whichever way the eye shall be turned, and this will sadden the heart. It cannot but lead to the following deep and solemn reflection: Here is the end of mortality. In a short time, I too, must become a co-tenant in this domain, and visitors will look upon my grave as I now look upon the graves of others. [8]

This sentiment was also communicated visually, as in angels flopped over monuments in agonizing despair, and ominous symbols and warnings in cemetery artwork.

But, by and large, there'd be few headstones in the cemetery with skull and crossbones or death's-heads, symbols of choice for Puritans and other God-fearing faithful who insisted the dead belonged in nasty little plots where the Devil tended his business. When you were dead, thought these fearmongers, indeed it was all over, and you were on your own, God be with you.

The new attitude acknowledged that, of course, the one you loved was dead, but also asked the question: What better place for both of you than the new cemeteries — they at eternal rest and you remembering them in a beautiful park? Here hope might truly spring eternal (or at least you could suspend disbelief for a few hours and enjoy the scenery). Religious considerations aside, who wouldn't appreciate a new burial ground that doubled as a professionally landscaped park? But death's sting transcends the ages, and not everyone was able to switch from grief to transcendent euphoria just because a loved one was buried in pleasant surroundings.

The Victorian element shaped the new cemeteries to a large degree. Children's graves are marked by statues of lambs and floppy-winged angels carrying tots off to the Pearly Gates. Pensive angels guarding mausoleums gaze skyward. The excessive ornamentation was designed as much to show "this-is-who-I-am" as to display sentiment. It was not to be forgotten just who was buried in these prestigious cemeteries; they emerged as showcases for the rich and prestigious. Many became inundated with artwork and crowded with mausoleums as society folk tried to outdo each other. Some started calling them "Ornamental" or "Sculpture" cemeteries. Gaudy and maudlin artwork — furniture, carved flowers, bas-reliefs on carved stone — dominated the landscape, squeezing nature out of the picture, which may have been all right for some but disturbed those who saw the cemetery as a kind of preserve, where art should embellish, but not overwhelm, the landscape. "Social distinctions soon threatened the cemetery's democracy . . . ," notes *The Last Great Necessity*. "The most prominent monuments were soon noted in newspapers and cemetery guidebooks. Many proprietors also hired gardeners . . . Parts of the cemetery resembled a royal British estate . . ." [9] Some cemetery officials fought this indulgence by restricting what lot-owners could erect and opening up the grounds in a lawn scheme that gave the land room to breathe.

At the same time some cemeteries became elitist, some took pains to memorialize the poor and victims of tragedy. Green-Wood erected a large monument to the memory of 300 people killed in a theater fire in the late 1800s, and Mount Auburn permitted the poor to bury their own in the public lot.

The Modern Mausoleum

The American mausoleum has evolved — or regressed, depending on your viewpoint — from showcase architecture, the ultimate postmortem display of the rich, to the communal tomb for hundreds, if not thousands, of bodies. Thousands of "community" mausoleums have been built in the second half of the twentieth century, and hundreds of new ones go up each year. A subindustry of architects and builders for years has been a staple of the supplier trade of America's $4-billion cemetery industry. Chances are you'll get a call one of these days from a telemarketer or door-to-door cemetery "prospector" looking to sell someone at your home a space in the wall in the town's mausoleum-under-construction.

You'll find a few modern temple mausoleums here and there, but by and large today's mausoleums are sweeping rectangular buildings, space-savers and money-makers for cemeteries using limited land to provide as

many "interments" (referring to burials or entombments) as possible. Going out in a mausoleum crypt has taken its place, along with cremation, as America's chief burial alternative.

The rise of the community mausoleum parallels the rise of the crowded cemetery, which has come full circle from the days of the late eighteenth century, when overcrowded graveyards spurred development of the rural cemetery. America still has plenty of open space, despite sprawling urban populations and the omnipresent suburban strip mall landscape. But most people don't think it should be used for dead bodies. There are enough of us in the ground already, this thinking goes. As cemeteries' burial space dwindles, adjacent land cannot always be developed because of opposition from preservationists, environmentalists, property owners and others. People fight cemetery expansion as they might fight sewage treatment plants or hazardous waste dumps: Who wants one in their backyard?

The situation is acute in major urban areas, like New York City, where there's little if any grave space at most cemeteries — although there's plenty on Long Island and in Westchester County. There are notable exceptions, like Cincinnati's Spring Grove Cemetery, a rambling 750-acre park with room to bury an average of a few people a day well into the twenty-first century. Rose Hills Memorial Park in the Whittier section of Los Angeles has about 1,700 acres, much of it undeveloped.

New York City's Woodlawn Cemetery, on the other hand, has precious little burial space left, but hopes to buy back or assume ownership of several thousand unused graves in abandoned family and society plots. Many of these chunks of land were bought in the nineteenth and early twentieth centuries for extended families — graves for every member. As time went by, heirs moved away, decided to get cremated, or simply weren't interested in the family's little piece of real estate in the cemetery, just as it seems many are no longer interested in unoccupied crypts in family mausoleums. Woodlawn also has its eye on communal plots, like the YMCA's burial section, about half-filled, with space for another 100 or so graves — apparently reserved for no one in particular.

Unfortunately for Woodlawn, a New York State law forbids the resale or assumption of ownership of graves, due to what's considered the right of the grave itself never to be disturbed, occupied or not. Other states, on the other hand, allow cemeteries to repossess graves after fifty or seventy-five years have passed and no one's heard

from heirs of plot-owners. The New York State cemetery lobby has been working hard in recent years to get
the law overturned.

Enter the Community Mausoleum

The community mausoleum has become the logical
solution to America's latest burial crunch. It also makes
perfect economic sense, providing crypts for many
bodies and the revenue that goes with it, in a given
space that would formerly have provided just a few
burials. Today's mausoleums are similar to those of the
elite described earlier in that they are composed of
"crypt banks" or walls, with crypts stacked on top of
each other in rows, with as many as seven crypts per
row. There are more crypts in the modern mausoleum,
which now houses the remains of the community at
large, not just of one family, although private "family"
rooms within community mausoleums are not
uncommon.

A working formula for a cemetery erecting a mausoleum is about $750 per crypt; crypts usually sell for a
few thousand dollars each, depending on location. The
prime spot is eye-level, the middle tier, because there's
no bending, stooping or reaching to touch the shiny
marble "crypt front" or place a flower in the vase-hold-
er attached to the crypt handle — unlike upper-tier
crypts, 15 or 20 feet high, where you need the mausoleum hydraulic "casket lift" (or a ladder) to get eye-
level with your loved one's remains.

Contemporary mausoleums come in all shapes and
sizes, but the majority are community units with hundreds, if not thousands, of crypts. Few compare in crafts-
manship and beauty to the masterpieces in this book,
but most maintain tasteful architectural elements — if
only on the inside — in their role as collective indoor
tombs for the masses.

You'll find nondescript pillboxes, two or three stories high, plunked down in the middle of an unre-
markable cemetery, and sprawling modern designs with
floors and walls of marble, granite and stone. Mosaic
crypt front murals have become popular and can turn
a wall of crypts into artwork. Foyers are often decorated with statuary and paintings. There are stained glass
windows, gazebos in courtyards for meditative strolls,
and so on. At "chapel" mausoleums, the dead are prayed
for during services in the spirit of early Christians
praying for saints in martyriums.

Ingram Construction of Madison, Mississippi, a
major mausoleum builder, erected a few typical structures in 1990. The mausoleum at Prince George
Cemetery in Petersburg, Virginia, is an open-air rectangular "garden" mausoleum with 300 crypts sandwiched
between "end walls faced with native fieldstone and
shutters of red polished granite," according to *American
Cemetery* magazine. Also in 1990, Ingram built a 560-
crypt "hillside chapel mausoleum" — another long, rectangular structure — next to another chapel mausoleum
in Russell Memorial Cemetery in Lebanon, Virginia.
"Most of the crypts," *American Cemetery* wrote, "will be
inside and will have Botticino polished marble shutters
and Verde Alps polished marble trim. A faceted glass
window will be a feature of the rear of the chapel . . .
Exterior crypts will have Sardinian pink polished granite shutters and Spanish black trim."

Another modern mausoleum builder, McCleskey
Mausoleum Associates of Norcross, Georgia, has been at
work since 1982 on a massive mausoleum in
Poughkeepsie (New York) Rural Cemetery. Nearly complete at the end of 1996 was phase four: a two-story affair
with a chapel on each floor — both trimmed in Alga
Marina marble and Verde Aver — with a facade of polished and "flame-finished" Barre granite. The crypt count
here is a precise 2,972, with 1,208 "cremation niches."

Most contemporary mausoleums are minuscule
compared with some of the monsters in our major
cities. Here's a description of a project at Inglewood
Park Cemetery in Los Angeles, from the July 1993
American Cemetery: "A seven-level high mausoleum contains 1,602 crypts, featuring Luna Pearl polished granite
shutters and Ebony Black polished granite trim. This is
the first phase of a 13,186-casket space project."
Inglewood is America's reigning king of the community mausoleum. By the turn of the century, it will have
some 100,000 crypts in more than a dozen mausoleums
and a budget-crypt section in a den of "catacombs"
called Capistrano Gardens under the cemetery's parking
lots. Inglewood's crypt-consciousness was raised over the
years as its efforts to expand were thwarted by local
authorities. Its most ambitious project, the recently completed Sunset Mission mausoleum, has 30,000 crypts.
Inglewood's Manchester Garden mausoleum comes a
close second with 28,000 crypts in seven underground
and two aboveground levels. Visiting a loved one in one
of these high-rise tombs is not as simple as strolling out to
a grave, but elevators whisk survivors up and down to
their loved one's spaces in the wall.

INTERIOR HALLWAY

Queen of Heaven Mausoleum
Chicago, Illinois

Queen of Heaven mausoleum, the world's largest Catholic mausoleum, contains a stunning display of artwork. Within its chapel, hallways and crypt rooms are 217 stained glass windows, dozens of statues, intricate mosaics, exotic hardwoods and 48 types of marble.

Queen of Heaven, King of the Mausoleum

Chicago's king of mausoleums is the Queen of Heaven triplex, the world's largest Catholic mausoleum, with 24,344 bodies (as of summer 1996) in its walls and another 9,000 empty crypts to be filled. The original mausoleum on the grounds of Queen of Heaven Cemetery was finished in 1956. Two years earlier, Chicago archbishop Samuel Cardinal Stritch announced that work would soon begin on the mausoleum, and asked if parishioners reaching their final days would consider buying a crypt to help finance the project. "We hope," wrote the archbishop in a letter to clergy and parishioners, "that many of our Catholic people who plan to select crypts in this mausoleum will avail themselves of the special advantages that accompany pre-completion purchases."[10] (In other words, buy before you die, and save.)

Queen of Heaven was a smashing success. Space sold quickly; by 1961 there was a new section, Queen of Angels, and in 1964 came Queen of All Saints, the last and final stage. The triplex is a fortresslike sandstone building with sharp curves in a near semicircle, dominated by a central entrance that rises to a 70-foot-high square Gothic tower, topped with ornate spires. On the entablature, in giant letters no one is likely to miss, is the fittingly prophetic announcement: "The Trumpet Shall Sound . . . The Dead Shall Rise."

Inside are 217 stained glass windows and perhaps 100 statues — and it should be added — at least during summer months, a host of the tiny and pesty phorid flies, *Megaselia scalaris*, the nemesis of many a mausoleum-tender. They are, however, easily swatted off and forgotten as you take in separate crypt rooms off long, carpeted hallways punctuated with nondescript couches and lamps on little tables.

An elevator shuttles visitors to three levels. The Chapel of Our Lady, a converted crypt section, includes "Willet" windows, made from lead castings with gold overlay, inside and outside, "so one sees the same thing on both sides of the window," as a Queen of Heaven brochure explains. There are shrines, like one to Our Lady of Fatima, made of marble fused with Venetian mosaics, one of the forty-eight types here, including a specialty shipped in from Antarctica. Framed on the walls are holy relics from Rome — remains of saints — from tombs erected after the fall of the Roman Empire and the decline of the mausoleum of antiquity.

SCHOENHOFEN MAUSOLEUM
Graceland Cemetery
Chicago, Illinois

Janusz, an eighteen-year-old high school student from Tarnow, Poland, installs weatherstripping on the Schoenhofen mausoleum as part of Graceland Cemetery's program of perpetual care for mausoleums.

The Schoenhofen mausoleum is an example of an adaptation of the mausoleum at the Cimitero Monumentale in Milan, Italy. The mausoleum is the final resting place of Prussian-born brewer Peter Schoenhofen (1827–1893).

STAINED GLASS RESTORATION
Cypress Lawn Memorial Park
Colma, California

Michael Jimenez, curator of stained glass at Cypress Lawn Memorial Park, holds a recently restored panel of stained glass from Cypress Lawn's catacombs. Cypress Lawn has a separate building dedicated to stained glass restoration and monument and mausoleum repair.

VOODOO QUEEN TOMB
St. Louis Cemetery No. 1
New Orleans, Louisiana

(*Opposite*) This is the reputed burial place of one of New Orleans's most notorious Voodoo queens, Marie Laveau. The mystic cult of Voodooism has its origins in Africa, although it was brought to New Orleans by way of the Caribbean island of Santo Domingo. Voodoo developed quite a following in the nineteenth century and still exists today. There are always offerings of some sort in front of the tomb. The exterior of the tomb is awash in *X*'s, a voodoo sign for good luck. Guidebooks describe this tomb as "Greek Revival" — but at best, it is a rather stripped-down version of the style.

These brick and plaster "house-tombs" often contain the remains of generations of families. They are usually designed with two vaults, one above the other, and a pit or *caveau* underneath them. When room is needed for another body, the tomb is opened and the bones of the previous occupant are removed and placed in the caveau. In the past, caskets that had not completely disintegrated were used for firewood. Very practical, those New Orleaneans!

A Case for Appreciation

Here is an opportune space for the argument to be made for the preservation of the architectural masterpieces in this book. The truth is most of them are well preserved and most of the cemeteries themselves are beautifully manicured parks and arboretums. Our real case is for appreciation — appreciation of America's least appreciated architecture, the mausoleum.

It must first be said that some rural cemeteries have taken a beating over the years: toppled tombstones, decapitated statues, stolen and smashed stained glass mausoleum windows. One encounters pockets of vandalism, as in Oakwood Cemetery, in Syracuse, where

graffiti have ruined more than a few beautiful mausoleums. Some entrances of stunning mausoleums, like the Wieting "stupa" temple, are cemented shut with material completely out of character with the building. The Longstreet pyramid mausoleum serves as a shelter for partyers who light campfires at the base of its grafitti-besmirched door. In the fall of 1996, a Syracuse newspaper told of college beer parties at Oakwood before Saturday football games with their fallout of beer cans and debris.

It should also be said that there's a certain melancholy and fitting charm to a mausoleum that's been left to age within a cemetery's woodland, and has been committed to the earth, as its occupants have been committed to its crypts. Allegheny Cemetery's old brownstone Wharton mausoleum was built deep into the side of a hill many years ago and looks as if it's been slowly and inescapably swallowed up by the earth. It would seem to be robbing Allegheny's Moorhead mausoleum if the green plants sprouting from its dark and menacing Gothic dome were clipped off. And who would trim the branches massaging the angel atop Allegheny's stone temple Kaercher mausoleum?

Get Thee to a Cemetery

Despite free cemetery tours; despite write-ups in newspapers and magazines; despite promotion in tourist bureaus' "places-to-see" brochures; despite documentaries tracing the compelling history of our burial grounds; despite all this, attendance at rural cemeteries remains low. We found all but a few oddly devoid of humanity during breezy summer days (except New Orleans, where the humidity was as oppressive as one would expect). Cemetery officials tell us that getting people to visit is no easy task. Buffalo's Forest Lawn was a notable exception: A number of roller bladers, runners, cyclists and office workers on lunch breaks charged through the cemetery gates during our time there for their daily trek.

A lot has changed since these cemeteries were laid out in the nineteenth century, and it's clear there's much more to do with free time today than stroll though a cemetery. But we hope these pages will make the cemetery-shy reconsider. There's no charge to enter these gates, no one will bother you there, and nowhere else will you find the architecture of eternity.

Notes

1. Peter Hellman, "Where History Is at Rest," *New York Times*, Sept. 6, 1996, page C-1.

2. Howard Montagu Colvin, *Architecture and the Afterlife* (New Haven: Yale University Press, 1991).

3. See note 2 above.

4. See note 2 above.

5. Barbara Rotundo, "Mount Auburn Cemetery: A Proper Boston Institution," *Harvard Library Bulletin*, vol. 22, no. 3 (July 1974).

6. See note 5 above.

7. *Cemetery of Spring Grove: Its Charter, Rules and Regulations* (Cincinnati: Gazette Office, Wright, Fisher and Co., 1989).

8. See note 7 above.

9. David Charles Sloane, *The Last Great Necessity: Cemeteries in American History* (Baltimore: Johns Hopkins University Press, 1955).

10. *Queen of Heaven Mausoleum* (a booklet published by the Archdiocese of Chicago, 1954).

MILITARY CEMETERY

The Presidio
San Francisco, California

(*On pages 26–27*) When most rural cemeteries were founded, they were located outside city limits, but still an easy carriage ride away. As cities grew, they soon surrounded cemeteries, effectively transforming them into urban rather than rural cemeteries.

In 1901, San Franciscans banned burial within their city limits, and in 1914 Mayor "Sunny" Jim Rolph signed a bill providing for the ultimate removal of all cemeteries from the city. For months, long lines of hearses transported the disinterred dead south to the now booming necropolis of Colma.

But the Presidio's military cemetery, with its magnificent views of the Golden Gate Bridge, remained untouched and was allowed to continue as an active cemetery. Burials are still conducted at the Presidio, even though the Presidio itself is no longer an active military base.

REVIVAL ARCHITECTURAL STYLES

The Past Becomes the Present

Revival styles of architecture dominated nineteenth-century building in America. In fact, it was not until the end of the nineteenth century that any other architectural style gained more than a foothold. Even progressive architects, such as Henry Hobson Richardson, found inspiration in the past and combined historic architectural styles with new forms of their own design. Richardson's fusion of Romanesque architecture with his own ideas created the heavily rusticated "Richardsonian Romanesque" architecture found in many late nineteenth-century government buildings.

Excavations at Herculaneum and Pompeii in the mid-eighteenth century were big news in Europe. They quickly became a necessary part of one's "tour" of the continent. These excavations added to the already growing interest in all things ancient and fueled the revival of Classical, Romanesque, Gothic, Byzantine and Renaissance models in architecture.

In 1798, Napoleon invaded Egypt not only with his army, but also with scientists and artists. His military campaign was a disaster, but the artists and scientists who accompanied his troops produced volumes of material about this strange and mystical place. Egyptomania spread across Europe and quickly made its way to the

United States. The *Description de l'Égypte*, published in 1822, reported the findings of the artists and scientists who accompanied Napoleon on his Egyptian Campaign and provided additional inspiration to designers and architects. Egyptian Revival architecture, despite its pagan influences, found a ready market in the growing rural cemetery movement that was spreading across America.

Near the end of the nineteenth century, Chicago architect Louis Sullivan experimented with strong, angular forms and ornamental embellishments drawn from nature. His "Sullivanesque" architecture experienced a relatively short run of popularity before being quashed by Revival styles.

The Revival styles' second wind came just as Sullivan and other members of the Chicago School were making inroads in architectural taste. The 1893 Columbian Exhibition in Chicago discounted Sullivan's work and proclaimed a return to the classics. Revival styles, especially Classical Revival, enjoyed another thirty-year run before the emergence of Art Deco in the 1920s.

Mausoleum architects and builders based most of their designs on styles that were popular at the time. Any student of architecture need look no further than a big-city cemetery for a quick course in Revival architecture of the nineteenth and early twentieth centuries.

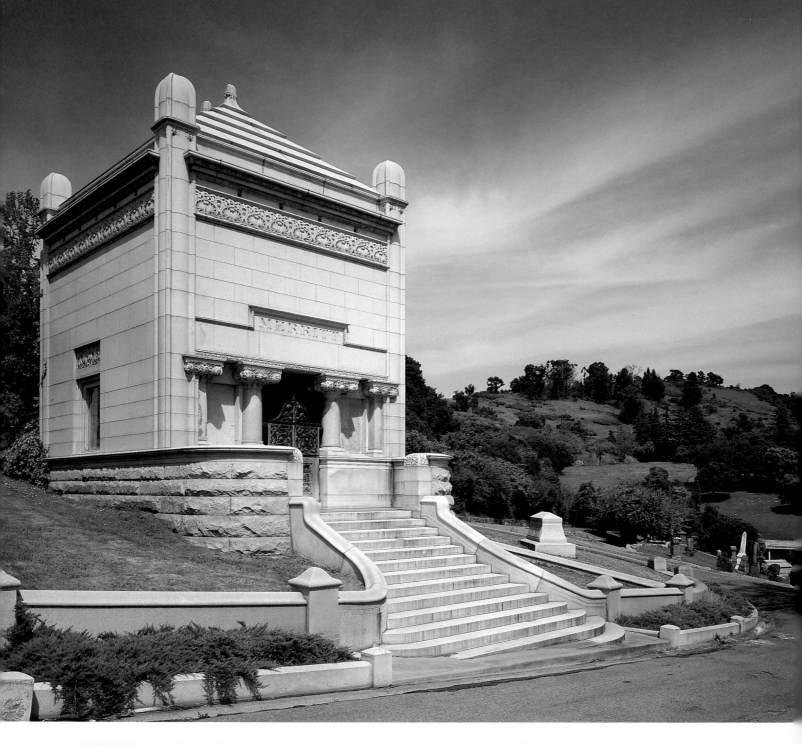

MERRITT MAUSOLEUM

Mountain View Cemetery
Oakland, California

❦

The Merritt mausoleum perches at the very top of Millionaires Row in Mountain View Cemetery. In form, the mausoleum is an unconventional temple. It must be considered a daring, high-style expression of the deceased's individuality. There is an interesting play of smooth and rough masonry, accented with delicately sculpted Romanesque ornament.

Dr. Samuel Merritt was one of the early residents and promoters of Oakland, California — among other things, a lake, a hospital and a college are named after him today. He served as mayor of Oakland in 1868, was a regent of the University of California and founded the Oakland Savings Bank and the California Insurance Company. Trained as a physician, he apparently didn't look after his own health. The 340-pound Merritt died in 1890 of diabetes, complicated by uremic poisoning.

EHRET MAUSOLEUM
Woodlawn Cemetery
Bronx, New York

(*Right*) Authoritative stone lions guard the Romanesque Revival mausoleum of George Ehret (d. 1927). Hallmarks of Romanesque architecture, as seen in the Ehret mausoleum, are the massive scale, squared-off surfaces, a portico with a recessed, rounded arch, and the use of architectural carving and sculpture typified by the swagged floral decorations in heavy relief. The Ehret mausoleum, built around 1899, contains 56 crypts, 28 on each side.

GHIRARDELLI MAUSOLEUM
Lower Tier, Millionaires Row
Mountain View Cemetery
Oakland, California

(*Below*) If you wanted to make a final statement about how wealthy you were in the San Francisco Bay Area, you chose a site in Millionaires Row in Oakland's Mountain View Cemetery. Domenico "Domingo" Ghirardelli, whose name has become synonymous with fine chocolate, made such a choice. On the right is the Ghirardelli family mausoleum.

The Ghirardelli family plot was originally in St. Mary's Catholic Cemetery, adjacent to Mountain View. According to local legend, Domingo Ghirardelli's young granddaughter Aurelia became gravely ill in 1879, and a priest refused her last rites (speculation is that the Ghirardelli family were behind in their tithe payments).

Thus, young Aurelia died without receiving the sacraments. This so enraged Ghirardelli that he forbade any members of his family to enter a Catholic church again.

In 1890, Domingo Ghirardelli had the mausoleum in the photograph constructed at Mountain View. Then, one night, he and his sons took a wagon to St. Mary's Cemetery, removed the four bodies from the Ghirardelli tomb and transported and reinterred them at Mountain View. As a further slap in the face of the Catholic church, Ghirardelli had a most un-Catholic Masonic emblem carved above the mausoleum's entrance.

Note the hourglass with wings beneath the sculpted mourning woman. This graphically symbolizes how time flies, and, therefore, that life should be lived to the fullest. The severe lines of this structure are essentially Egyptian Revival, especially the battered shape of the entry. The Ghirardelli mausoleum is basically a pedestal for the weeping woman sculpture rather than a fully realized building.

KAERCHER MAUSOLEUM

Allegheny Cemetery
Pittsburgh, Pennsylvania

(*Opposite, top left*) It won't be long until this little Classical Revival mausoleum, c. 1860, is completely engulfed by foliage. The mausoleum was built for John Kaercher, one of the owners of the tanning firm C. Kaercher & Sons. A number of members of the Kaercher family are entombed here, but in the 1980s ol' Doc Kaercher informed the cemetery board, "I'm the last of the line. After I've passed on, seal it up."

And so they did.

BOURNE MAUSOLEUM

Mount Auburn Cemetery
Cambridge, Massachusetts

(*Opposite, top right*) Massive and imposing, the Bourne Romanesque Revival mausoleum looks as though it's here to stay. Ornamentation is almost nonexistent, except for an oversized keystone worked into the doorway and a few round sandstone caps that look like stone porthole covers. Hallmarks of Romanesque Revival architecture, as seen in the Bourne mausoleum, are the heavy buttresses and a rounded arch with a deep reveal forming the entry.

BRUNSWIG MAUSOLEUM

Metairie Cemetery
New Orleans, Louisiana

(*Above*) Most large metropolitan cemeteries sport a pyramid or two. A number of cemeteries also contain a variation on the type of pyramid found at the Brunswig mausoleum. The design of the Brunswig mausoleum has been attributed to a tomb in the Cimitero Monumentale in Milan, Italy. These pyramids are usually constructed with smooth granite sides, a sphinx and some sort of human figure. At the Brunswig mausoleum, the human figure is a female with a libation urn. Since Egyptian architecture is pagan in origin, most mausoleum designers added Christian symbols to appease those who believed cemeteries should be places celebrating traditional religious values, not pagan deities.

Lucien Brunswig, who is spending eternity in the style of the pharaohs, was the head of a large wholesale drug firm.

WHARTON MAUSOLEUM

Allegheny Cemetery
Pittsburgh, Pennsylvania

(*Opposite, bottom*) The Wharton mausoleum, built c. 1860, seems to be comfortably burrowing into the hillside. The mausoleum's rich patina has been aided, no doubt, by decades of exposure to the smokestacks of Pittsburgh's many industries. A blooming "snowball" bush softens and completes the scene. The Wharton mausoleum's form is Classical Revival, with some early Victorian embellishments. One can easily imagine the mausoleum's double doors gracing the parlor of a fashionable Pittsburgh address.

The lot owner and one of the occupants of the mausoleum was Oliverette Wharton, a relative of the Wharton brothers, who owned the Ormsby Ironworks in Pittsburgh.

BODMANN MAUSOLEUM
Spring Grove Cemetery
Cincinnati, Ohio

(*Left*) H. Q. French of New York designed this perfect little Gothic Revival mausoleum in the form of an aedicule, a miniature building in the shape of a church. There is an interesting play of smooth and rusticated stone; Gothic arches frame stained glass windows; a splash of rose-colored granite is used on the columns to contrast with the gray stone. Quatrefoils on the upper windows and the door add balance. Enhancing the fairy-tale appeal of the Bodmann mausoleum is its beautiful setting in relationship to its environment.

Much of the beauty of Spring Grove Cemetery can be attributed to landscape architect Adolph Strauch. Strauch was born in 1822 in the Prussian province of Silesia. He studied botany and in 1838 took a job in the Imperial Gardens in Vienna. It was there that he developed his taste for well-groomed lawns carefully framed by masses of trees and sculpted ponds. In 1848 he worked in London's Royal Botanical Gardens and later guided foreign visitors through the Crystal Palace Exhibition. During one of these tours, a man from Cincinnati, Robert Bonner Bowler, gave him his calling card and instructed Strauch to look him up if he were ever in Cincinnati. As luck would have it, in 1852, while Strauch was touring America, he missed a train from Texas to Niagara Falls and found himself in Cincinnati. He looked up Bowler, who introduced Strauch to a number of wealthy friends. In short order, Strauch was designing gardens and landscapes all over Cincinnati. In 1854 Strauch was offered the superintendent's job at Spring Grove, a post he held until his death in 1883.

GARRISON MAUSOLEUM
Green-Wood Cemetery
Brooklyn, New York

(*Opposite*) This Byzantine/Turkish Revival mausoleum is the final port of call for Commodore C. K. Garrison (1809–85). Garrison's tomb was designed by New York architect Griffith Thomas, who also designed a number of buildings in New York City, including the original New York Life Insurance Building. For the Garrison mausoleum, Thomas worked with Islamic and Moorish forms, topping his creation with a dome that one can easily imagine transported straight from a mosque in Istanbul. Of particular interest is the way the polychrome granite treatment is used to draw attention to the different architectural elements.

Garrison's title of "Commodore" was largely honorary: Rather than piloting ships, he was in the much more lucrative business of owning them. It appears his highly successful steamship line, which traded goods with Australia and the Orient, had a strong influence on the design of his mausoleum.

MURPHY MAUSOLEUM
Cypress Lawn Memorial Park
Colma, California

The design of the Murphy mausoleum, built of sand-stone in 1921, has been attributed to Bernard J. S. Cahill (1866–1944), who designed a number of structures at Cypress Lawn. Cahill chose French Gothic, a style of architecture that emerged with the construction of twelfth- and thirteenth-century French cathedrals. The term *Gothic* was originally intended by Italian Renaissance artists to be pejorative. When compared to Renaissance buildings, medieval cathedrals were thought to be so crude that only a "barbarian" Goth could have produced them. The Goths were Germanic people who had sacked Rome in A.D. 410.

The Murphy mausoleum is reminiscent of the Chapel of St. Hubert in the city of Amboise, in the Loire valley in France. The Chapel of St. Hubert was also used as a model for the Belmont mausoleum at Woodlawn cemetery in the Bronx (see page 81).

ROBINSON MAUSOLEUM
Spring Grove Cemetery
Cincinnati, Ohio

John Robinson built this mausoleum in 1874 for $35,000. Although the basic form of the mausoleum is a Gothic Revival cruciform, the heavily rusticated blue limestone walls reflect a Romanesque influence. To contrast with the rough surface of blue limestone, the architect chose marble for the mauseleum's smooth surfaces. Statues of Faith, Hope and Charity frame the entry, while the Archangel Gabriel, surmounting the dome, has his horn ready to signal to the heavens the impending arrival of another Robinson.

The Robinson family owned Robinson's Circus from 1824 until 1916, when they sold it to the American Circus. It was subsequently merged with Ringling Brothers.

E. J. "LUCKY" BALDWIN MAUSOLEUM

Cypress Lawn Memorial Park
Colma, California

This mausoleum is probably exactly what most people imagine a family tomb should look like. Its Classical style is admirable for its restrained elegance and enduring beauty. Twin polished black marble columns in Tuscan style frame the entry. A ray of sunlight illuminates a figurative stained glass window and, crowning the pediment, an eternal flame in black marble.

Like many of his generation, Elias J. Baldwin (1828–1909) made his fortune as a Gold Rush entrepreneur. He earned his nickname "Lucky" by speculating in the Comstock Lode silver mines of Nevada. He made his fortune selling out at peak value. Baldwin increased his fortune through successful endeavors in the hotel and real estate businesses. He built and owned major hotels in San Francisco and on Lake Tahoe. His most enduring legacy was his interest in the Santa Anita Rancho in Southern California, which eventually became the world-famous Santa Anita Raceway.

DE LA MONTANYA MAUSOLEUM

Cypress Lawn Memorial Park
Colma, California

Dark and brooding, the de la Montanya mausoleum is in a state of arrested decay. The mausoleum, designed in 1909 by noted funerary architect Bernard J. S. Cahill, is constructed of red sandstone and originally contained three Tiffany stained glass windows. Cahill modeled his three-stage Spanish Gothic tower on a cathedral in Burgos, Spain. Pinnacles, crockets, sprockets and gargoyles protrude from every surface, making this look more like an elaborate confection than a home for the dead.

Like many sandstone structures, it seems to attract ivy like a magnet. Ivy grows in the cracks and crevices of the stone, slowly forcing the joints apart. The problem is compounded in structures like this, which have a variety of surfaces to which the ivy may attach itself. As if damage from the ivy weren't enough, an earthquake in the late 1950s destroyed the Tiffany windows and seriously damaged the structure itself.

James de la Montanya (1819–1909) was one of many men who struck it rich during the California Gold Rush. And like most of those men, he made money not by digging for gold, but by selling supplies to those who did the digging. In addition to supplying the '49ers with hardware and other materials, de la Montanya developed a prosperous horse-breeding business.

CHAUNCEY MAUSOLEUM

Green-Wood Cemetery
Brooklyn, New York

Multicrocketed Gothic spires reach toward the heavens in what appears to be a boarded-up fairy-tale castle. The Chauncey family mausoleum, also known as the "Prisoner's Vault," was constructed during the Civil War by Confederate prisoners confined at Sing Sing Penitentiary.

By the 1860s Green-Wood Cemetery had become the place for prominent New Yorkers to be buried. An 1866 *New York Times* article observed, "It is the ambition of every New Yorker to live on Fifth Ave., take his airings in the [Central] Park, and to sleep with his fathers in Green-Wood."

FELTMAN MAUSOLEUM
Green-Wood Cemetery
Brooklyn, New York

The Archangel Michael, sword at the ready, tops the domed cupola of Charles Feltman's temple mausoleum. With Corinthian columns, cherubs, statuary, urns — you name it — the Feltman mausoleum could serve as a primer for any student of Classical architecture. Most municipalities would be happy to have a building as ornate as this decorate their town square, but this edifice serves to celebrate only one man.

Feltman, a pie maker/baker, owned a push cart on New York's Coney Island. His pies weren't doing so well, and he couldn't seem to compete with the inns on Coney Island selling hot dishes. Feltman pondered, finally returning to a memory in his youth of a long, slightly curved sausage, known as a dachshund sausage, that the butcher's guild in Frankfurt, Germany, had popularized. A lightbulb went off in his head; he abandoned the pie business and concentrated on selling frankfurter sandwiches. His cart was small, with only enough room for his frankfurter sandwiches and two condiments, mustard and sauerkraut. His simple idea was an instant success; shortly thereafter he opened Feltman's German Beer Garden, complete with carousel, where he continued to sell his money-making franks.

Feltman was not the only one immortalized in American folklore because of these slender sausages. In 1913, Feltman hired Nathan Handwerker to help him for the princely sum of $11.00 a week. A few years later, two frankfurter aficionados, Jimmy Durante and Eddie Condon, irritated that Feltman had raised his price to 10 cents, convinced Nathan to open his own operation, selling them for 5 cents. Nathan promoted his frankfurters (made to wife Ida's recipe) by offering them free to doctors at nearby Coney Island Hospital on the condition that the docs consume them standing next to his stand while clad in hospital whites and wearing their stethoscopes. Another triumph for capitalism, and for Nathan, whose frankfurters and other meat products thrive to this day. Then there is the story of Harry Stevens, a concessionaire at New York baseball games. Supposedly, his vendors would call out, "Get your red-hot dachshund sausages!" and . . . well, you know the rest.

STEWART MAUSOLEUM

Green-Wood Cemetery
Brooklyn, New York

Noted architect Stanford White designed this mausoleum for the Stewart family. Although records do not indicate how many monuments and mausoleums White personally designed, his firm, McKim, Mead and White, produced forty funerary monuments between 1879 and 1919. Most of the firm's designs are Classical in origin and often the result of collaboration with other designers and sculptors.

White's rather austere design for the Stewart mausoleum is enhanced by bronze reliefs sculpted by Augustus Saint Gaudens. Saint Gaudens achieved fame as the designer of the U.S. twenty-dollar gold piece, often referred to simply as the "Saint Gaudens." The bronze panels Saint Gaudens crafted for the Stewart mausoleum are very low relief and look as if they have been scratched into the surface. One panel depicts an angel holding a banner or scroll, symbolizing taking inventory of one's life. The other panel presents an angel holding a long horn, representing the Archangel Gabriel, who proclaims to the heavens the impending

arrival of another soul. The angel is seated on a bench inscribed with a biblical verse.

The Stewart family mausoleum contains, among others, the remains of two-year-old John "Jackie" Gardner, who died in 1865 following a bout of pneumonia. Jackie was the son of Jack Gardner and Isabella Stewart Gardner. Isabella was a wealthy woman in her own right. She inherited a great deal of money from her father, David Stewart, who made his fortune from Pennsylvania ironworks.

To help relieve her depression over Jackie's untimely death, Isabella's doctor suggested a trip to Europe. During her trip, she further relieved her depression by purchasing Rembrandts, Vermeers, Titians and Botticellis. These beautiful works of art would later become the foundation of the Isabella Stewart Gardner Museum collection in Boston.

Isabella Stewart Gardener opened her "house museum" to the public, but brooded over it like a mother hen. In her later years, when bedridden, she would caution imaginary visitors not to touch her treasured works of art. Evidently she got over young Jackie's death, electing to be buried in Boston, close to her art collection, rather than in the family tomb in Brooklyn.

WIARDA MAUSOLEUM
Green-Wood Cemetery
Brooklyn, New York

Little is known about John C. Wiarda, except that he left to posterity this beautiful Classical Revival mausoleum. Building a mausoleum is certainly no guarantee that one will be remembered forever: The families of the deceased often move or break up, endowment funds for mausoleums dry up too, and try as they may, cemetery officials just can't seem to locate family members.

In many cemeteries, numerous plots have been bought and paid for, but plot-owners have long since vanished without telling family members or willing the plots to anyone. Many states have laws stipulating that unclaimed plots revert to the cemetery after a few decades.

In New York, where Green-Wood cemetery is located, there is no such law; plots are sold in perpetuity. Because of the shortage of land for burial space in metropolitan areas, cemeteries like Green-Wood are lobbying the government to modify the law so they can reclaim unused land and use it for new burials.

NIBLO MAUSOLEUM
Green-Wood Cemetery
Brooklyn, New York

Lions are, as everyone knows, ferocious beasts. The one guarding the Gothic Revival Niblo mausoleum seems to be toothless and rather forlorn. The Niblo mausoleum, comfortably nestled into the hillside and overlooking a small pond along Dale Avenue, is the picture of serenity and peace, but its history is anything but serene.

William "Billy" Niblo (1789–1878) took full advantage of his cemetery plot and liberally interpreted the idea that cemeteries were for the living. He hosted elaborate parties on the grounds in front of his mausoleum. These parties were an extension of his famous restaurant and theater complex on lower Broadway, known as "Niblo's Garden." The Garden was well known as the site of plays, featuring risqué extravaganzas with bare-legged dancers. One of Niblo's productions included 300 babies marching and crawling across a stage. Perhaps the lion is a refugee from one of Niblo's productions and that is why he looks so tired.

POTTER MAUSOLEUM

Graceland Cemetery
Chicago, Illinois

The Potter mausoleum, a classic example of Richard-sonian Romanesque architecture, has the look of a medieval fortress. It is rare for a single architect to be so influential in popularizing an architectural style that it is named after him, but so it was with Henry Hobson Richardson (1838–86).

The dominant architectural styles in the nineteenth century were revival styles (Classical Revival, Gothic Revival, Egyptian Revival, Renaissance Revival, etc.). Richardson added his own twist to Romanesque Revival style by advocating the use of heavily rusticated stone. Romanesque architecture usually uses smooth stone. Richardson also favored deep window reveals and cavernous door openings. The overall impression created by his buildings is one of heaviness. His style adapted well to large, authoritative structures, such as churches, university buildings, railroad stations, courthouses and, in this case, a mausoleum.

PALMER MONUMENT

Graceland Cemetery
Chicago, Illinois

Architects McKim, Mead and White designed this temple to shelter the twin sarcophagi of Potter Palmer (1826–1902) and his wife Bertha. Sixteen massive Ionic columns ring the structure and a line of antefixes stands at attention along the roof line. Both sarcophagi are embellished with flowery garlands and downturned torches, symbolizing life extinguished.

If all of this seems excessive, remember it was customary for wealthy late nineteenth-century Americans to display their wealth in a big way. Potter Palmer's fortune began with a store he opened on Lake Street in central Chicago. He instituted the practice of the "money-back guarantee." He even allowed customers to take items home on approval, try them out and bring them back if they weren't happy.

Eventually, he sold his store to Marshall Field and ventured into real estate. He bought Chicago's State Street, widened it and lined it with new buildings. The gem of his State Street collection of buildings was the Palmer House, a luxurious hotel which he presented to his young bride, Bertha Honore, as a wedding present. Much of State Street, including the Palmer House, was destroyed in the Great Chicago Fire of 1871. Undaunted, Palmer borrowed money and rebuilt the street, complete with a new and even more impressive Palmer House Hotel. He built a castle for Bertha on Lake Shore Avenue, where she held court as the queen of Chicago society and collected French Impressionist paintings, which she later donated to the Art Institute of Chicago.

VAN NESS/PARSONS MAUSOLEUM
Green-Wood Cemetery
Brooklyn, New York

Another pyramidal mausoleum that appears to have its inspiration in the Cimitero Monumentale in Milan, Italy, is the Van Ness/Parsons mausoleum. The mausoleum presents a confusion of pagan and Christian symbology, including a grouping of a sphinx with a figure of Christ holding a lamb, as well as two female figures (one is out of view in this photo) displaying infants. Gracing the bronze door is a further religious anomaly — a crucifix superimposed over a zodiacal circle of the planets and the sun. Completing the tableau, carved into the cavetto cornice, are vulture wings, twin cobras and a sun. Little is known about the Van Ness/Parsons family, but their mausoleum certainly arouses one's curiosity.

LETCHWORTH MAUSOLEUM
Forest Lawn Cemetery
Buffalo, New York

The July 12, 1872, issue of the *Buffalo Commercial Advertiser & Journal* noted: "Josiah Letchworth has erected what will be, when finished, the most elegant mausoleum in the country. The outside walls are of Medina and Connecticut brown sandstone. The inside walls and ceiling are of the most beautiful varieties of Italian and Egyptian marble finished in elegant and appropriate style."

Apparently, Josiah was overcome with grief when Mary (1839–68), his bride of only three years, passed away while touring Switzerland. He spent close to $100,000 on this Classical Revival mausoleum. The centerpiece of the interior is a statue of his bride.

On the interior back wall of the mausoleum is an inscription that is as much a tribute to the run-on sentence as it is to Mary: "In memory of whom this monument and mausoleum have been erected by her husband whose unbounding love could not bind to earth the immortal spirit of her who was its most cherished object whose presence made earth a paradise, whose virtues, accomplishments and nobility of heart while they won the homage they deserved were excelled by a living Christian faith which even in her death taught the heart to say, 'even so, Father, for so it seemed good in thy sight.'" How monumentally Josiah must have loved his Mary!

MACKAY MAUSOLEUM
Green-Wood Cemetery
Brooklyn, New York

Guidebooks printed in 1901 estimated the cost of the Mackay mausoleum, dedicated in 1898, at $100,000. Other sources believed the cost to be as high as $300,000—a tidy sum. Irish immigrant John William Mackay (1831–1902) could well afford his stone fortress. Mackay was one of the so-called Silver Kings who developed and prospered from Nevada's rich Comstock Lode. He arrived in Virginia City, the center of the Comstock Lode, in 1859. By 1868, through hard work and shrewd investment, he had amassed a small fortune and was a partner in the Kentuck mine.

He formed a partnership, known as the Bonanza Associates, with three other Irishmen, James Fair, James Flood and William O'Brien; a few years later the partners opened a mining deposit that came to be known as the "Big Bonanza" (remember Ben Cartright and his sons Adam, Hoss and Little Joe?). Mackay was suddenly one of the richest men in the country. Not content to be merely a "Silver King," he tackled the likes of wily businessman Jay Gould. Mackay eventually broke Gould's Western Union Telegraph monopoly by establishing the Postal Telegraph and Cable Corporation.

The name of the designer of the Mackay mausoleum is not known. The mausoleum, however, is reminiscent of the Baroque designs of seventeenth-century English architect, John Vanbrugh, the designer of Castle Howard and Blenheim Palace. Interesting features of the mausoleum are four bronze figures, manufactured in Munich, representing Sorrow, Faith, Death and Life, and the huge 40-ton roof stone, said to be the the largest piece of stone ever quarried in the United States. A highly unusual aspect of the Mackay mausoleum is that it was equipped with both heating and electrical systems. Plans for the mausoleum called for the installation of a favorite novelty at the Mackay estate — a stuffed moose that ran electrically on a track and was used for target practice. Alas, the plan never materialized and the moose rests elsewhere. Among 22 crypts lies the body of John Mackay's son, Clarence Mackay (1874–1938), best known as the father-in-law of composer Irving Berlin.

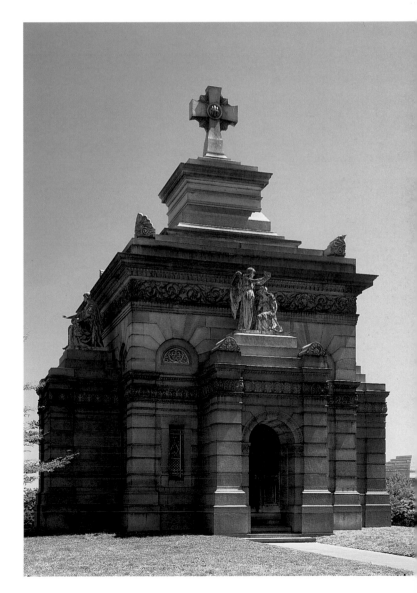

POTH MAUSOLEUM
West Laurel Hill Cemetery
Bala Cynwyd, Pennsylvania

The Poth mausoleum is a Classical Revival showcase featuring a flowery topped dome punctuated with a stylized pineapple, antefixes on every corner, Corinthian columns, stained glass above the door, dentils, twin bronze-capped urns, wreaths and more. All of this ornament seems fitting for a baron, even if he was a "beer baron."

Frederick August Poth (1840–1905) was born in Germany and came to Philadelphia in 1861. By 1863 he had married and set up a small brewery in his backyard. Mr. Poth possessed both business acumen and good brewing recipes. By 1875, F. A. Poth and Sons was the largest brewery in the United States, a claim it maintained until Poth's death in 1905. In addition to his brewery, Poth was quite active in real estate, acquiring and developing properties in the Parkside Avenue, Viola Street and Memorial Hall areas of Philadelphia.

BETZ MAUSOLEUM
West Laurel Hill Cemetery
Bala Cynwyd, Pennsylvania

One of the largest mausoleums in West Laurel Hill Cemetery is the Classical Revival Betz mausoleum. Years of exposure to the elements have given its copper dome and bronze doors a rich patina. The pediment, pilasters, blind windows, urns and lofty angel are all Classical Revival fare. Inside the mausoleum is an elaborate spiral staircase leading down a flight to thirty underground crypts.

John F. Betz (1831–1908) was one of Philadelphia's beer barons. He also owned a number of real estate holdings in Philadelphia, New York and Stuttgart, Germany. The family estate, Betzwood, which was sold following his death, later became famous as Lubin Studios, the world's largest silent movie studio. Movie fans wishing to experience the pastoral beauty of Betzwood may want to secure a copy of a silent movie shot at the estate, *Tillie's Tomato Surprise,* starring popular movie star of the day Marie Dressler.

CHILDS AND BAEDER MAUSOLEUMS

Laurel Hill Cemetery
Philadelphia, Pennsylvania

Two Classical Revival mausoleums catch the first rays of the summer sun at Laurel Hill Cemetery. Both are in an area known as Millionaire's Circle, which contains a collection of monuments and mausoleums of rich and famous Philadelphians.

George William Childs made his fortune selling and publishing books and in 1864 became the publisher of the *Public Ledger*, Philadelphia's major newspaper. He was a consummate host, entertaining presidents (Grant, Hayes, Arthur and Cleveland) and writers (Emerson, Holmes and Longfellow) at his city and country estates.

Unfortunately, little is known about the Baeder mausoleum.

DRAKE MAUSOLEUM

West Laurel Hill Cemetery
Bala Cynwyd, Pennsylvania

Flying sphinxes seem ready to swoop down on unwelcome visitors at the Drake family mausoleum. As with most Egyptian Revival architecture, a few Greek and perhaps a few Classical motifs are thrown in for good measure. In Egyptian mythology, these stone guardians, or *shesep-ankth* (living statues), were always male, usually with a lion's body and a human head. In Greek mythology, however, sphinxes were female. Ironically, most Egyptian Revival mausoleums sport the Greek variety. Further relieving the cold, hard granite are the vulture wing and sun design carved above the entry, the rounded corners of the mausoleum and the lotus blossoms etched into the pilasters, as well as on the bronze door. The Drake mausoleum was originally at Laurel Hill Cemetery, but both bodies and mausoleum were moved to West Laurel Hill.

A number of Drakes and members of their extended family are entombed inside, including Thomas Drake Martinez Cardeza and his mother, Mrs. Charlotte Drake Martinez Cardeza. Thomas and Charlotte were survivors of an "unsinkable" ship that ran into an iceberg in April 1912. But Mrs. Cardeza's brush with death as a passenger on the *Titanic* was just another adventure for her. Her big game hunts in Asia and Africa were frequently described by newspapers of the day.

SATTERWHITE MONUMENT

Cave Hill Cemetery
Louisville, Kentucky

Dr. Preston Pope Satterwhite hired famed Philadelphia architect Horace Trumbauer to design a monument for his wife, Florence Brokaw Martin Satterwhite, who died in 1927 at the age of 61. Trumbauer based his design on the Classical Revival Temple of Love constructed by French architect Richard Mique (1728–94) for Marie Antoinette in the gardens of the Petit Trianon at Versailles. Mique, in turn, had based his design on the Roman Temple of Vesta at Tivoli, built in the first century B.C.

While Trumbauer worked with B. A. & G. N. Williams, stone contractors in New York City, on the fabrication of the Tennessee marble monument, Dr. Satterwhite busied himself with the selection and preparation of the site. He selected a 26,343-square-foot site at Cave Hill, which he purchased for $50,000. Then he hired Wadley and Smythe, landscape contractors of New

York City, to prepare the site. Wadley and Smythe promptly ordered four freight cars of plantings, which arrived in Louisville in the spring of 1928. On June 18, 1928, the monument was officially declared finished.

Florence Brokaw Martin Satterwhite was born into a wealthy family. The Brokaw family had done well as clothiers and provided young Florence with a taste for the finer things in life. Her first marriage to Standard Oil Company executive James E. Martin ended when he died tragically in 1905 at age 59. He and his son were racing through New York City's streets when his car overturned. Florence inherited a considerable estate.

In 1908 she married Dr. Satterwhite. They also enjoyed a lavish lifestyle, dividing their time between New York and Palm Beach. Although the Satterwhites did not live in Louisville, Dr. Satterwhite, like his father and grandfather, studied medicine in Kentucky. After his studies, he set up his surgical practice in New York. Dr. Satterwhite donated considerable money to the J. B. Speed Art Museum in Louisville and to Cave Hill Cemetery.

IRVIN MAUSOLEUM

Cave Hill Cemetery
Louisville, Kentucky

Noted Louisville architect Henry Whitestone designed this modified Gothic Revival mausoleum for James F. Irvin in 1867. Whitestone drew his inspiration from the Greffult family mausoleum designed by A. T. Brongniart c.1816, in Père Lachaise Cemetery in Paris. A description of the Irvin mausoleum appeared in the April 16, 1871, edition of *The Louisville Daily Commercial*. The newspaper described the "Scotch granite" columns, dome and exterior walls and noted the different varieties of marble used on the interior surfaces. The newspaper went on to describe the crypts as "four depositories for coffins, with marble doors, awaiting their inmates."

Captain James E. Irvin (1812–83) made his fortune as a steamboat captain on the Ohio River. He was also on the cemetery board of Cave Hill Cemetery. This connection no doubt assured him one of the choice hilltop lots as his burial site. Sharing the mausoleum with Captain Irvin are his wife, Florence McHarry, and Florence's father, Frank McHarry.

Frank McHarry was originally buried in a tomb overlooking the Ohio River so that, legend has it, he could hurl curses at passing steamboats. Apparently, McHarry, who operated a ferry service on the river, had a long-standing feud with steamboats and even in death wanted the opportunity to voice a ghostly epithet. Another part of the story speculates that McHarry was buried standing up, but such is the stuff of legends. What is true is that his body is now quite horizontal in the Irvin mausoleum — out of earshot of those pesky steamboats.

LONGSTREET MAUSOLEUM
Oakwood Cemetery
Syracuse, New York

This towering pyramid, now sealed for all time, holds the remains of members of the Longstreet family. Cornelius Tyler Longstreet (1814–81), who built the mausoleum, was a successful merchant in the wholesale clothing trade. He also served on the board of directors of two Syracuse banks. Initially, Longstreet built a different mausoleum on this site. However, it did not fare well through the harsh upstate New York winters. So he went back to the drawing board and replaced it with this pyramid. The interior of the tomb once contained elegantly carved tablets, sculpture, furniture and a Persian rug. Unfortunately, the tomb has now been sealed, due to repeated vandalism.

LEWIS HENRY MORGAN MAUSOLEUM
Mount Hope Cemetery
Rochester, New York

Protruding from the hillside along Ravine Avenue in Rochester's Mount Hope Cemetery is the High Victorian Gothic mausoleum of Lewis Henry Morgan (1818–81). Lewis Henry Morgan's studies of the culture of the Seneca Indians earned him the title "father of the science of anthropology."

Like many sandstone mausoleums, this is slowly eroding, which somehow serves to enhance its brooding Gothic ornaments. The universal feature of all Gothic architecture is the pointed arch, seen here in the entry, and the fenestrations at the top of the twin steeples. The line of quatrefoils on the balustrade is also Gothic-inspired.

Mount Hope Cemetery, established in 1838, bills itself as America's first municipal Victorian cemetery. Among notables buried at Mount Hope are Frederick Douglass, Susan B. Anthony and the Bausch and Lomb families. Rochester's most famous citizen, George Eastman, who founded the Eastman Kodak Company, was cremated at Mount Hope, but his ashes lie beneath a giant cylindrical stone monument at the entrance to Kodak Park in Rochester.

GARVAN MAUSOLEUM

Woodlawn Cemetery
Bronx, New York

John Russell Pope designed this Ionic temple mausoleum for Francis P. Garvan. The Garvan mausoleum is rescued from being a fairly run-of-the-mill temple mausoleum by the two frieze panels, depicting mourners, that flank the double doors. These frieze panels were created by Edward Sanford, Jr., also responsible for most of the decorative sculpture in California's state capitol in Sacramento.

Francis P. Garvan (1875–1937) was appointed to the office of "Alien Property Custodian" by President Wilson during World War I. As part of his job, Garvan took it upon himself to confiscate a number of German patents. He believed doing so fit his job description. Then he sold these patents to the Chemical Foundation, Inc., a company of which he happened to be president. This looked fishy, so in 1922, when Wilson's successor, Warren G. Harding, took office, a full inquiry was instituted. This was followed by a well-publicized months-long trial. Amazingly, Garvan was cleared of any wrongdoing and the foundation, which had already made a considerable amount of money by licensing the use of the patents to American companies, was now in a position to subsidize the American Chemical Society, the National Research Council, chemical laboratories at leading universities and the publication of the bulletin *Chemical Abstracts*.

MARY BAKER EDDY MONUMENT
Mount Auburn Cemetery
Cambridge, Massachusetts

Often, monuments and mausoleums are designed by the same architect who designed other residences for the family. The Mary Baker Eddy monument did not follow this mold; instead, it was the result of a design competition. Egerton Swarthout, a New York architect, won the competition in 1914, with a tholos-form design of a circular colonnade consisting of eight columns, each 15 feet high. Swarthout omitted a roof because he felt there should be "nothing between the grave and sky but flowers."

Originally, the architect specified the monument be constructed of Colorado or Vermont white marble. In recognition of the harsh New England winters, however, Bethel (Vermont) white granite was substituted; granite, although harder to work, withstands the elements significantly better than marble.

The Mary Baker Eddy monument has been acknowledged to be one of the finest examples of the granite carver's craft. Among the details incorporated in the design are the wild rose, Mrs. Eddy's favorite flower, the morning glory, which opens to light and closes to darkness, the lamp of wisdom and a sheaf of wheat. Mary Baker Eddy (1821–1910) was the "discoverer" and founder of Christian Science. The inscriptions on the memorial are from the Bible and Mrs. Eddy's teachings.

WARNER MAUSOLEUM
Woodlawn Cemetery
Bronx, New York

(*Left*) Dozens of antefixes protrude from the roof of the Warner mausoleum, built in 1893. The elegance of the mausoleum is further enhanced by the delicately sculpted Corinthian columns, a line of toothsome dentils under the eaves and cross-patterned ventilation windows. The Warners had ample time to enjoy their stylish mausoleum; Lucien C. Warner died in 1925, thirty-two years after the mausoleum's construction, and his wife, Keren S. Warner, died in 1933.

PORTER MAUSOLEUM
Woodlawn Cemetery
Bronx, New York

(*Right*) Modified Roman Doric columns march around the circular Porter mausoleum. Also ringing the mausoleum are two dozen winged cherub heads and an equal number of antefixes. Topping this majestic mausoleum is a flowery urn. The mausoleum was built in 1927 to house the remains of William H. Porter, who died in 1926. His wife, Esther J. Porter, joined him in their eternal home in 1934.

BASTIAN MAUSOLEUM

Woodlawn Cemetery
Bronx, New York

It is quite unusual to see a woman's name prominently carved on a mausoleum. After all, during the age of robber barons and millionaires, when most of the grand mausoleums were constructed, a woman's place was in the home, certainly not in making a name for herself,

except, of course, with her husband's approval. So who was Elisabeth Bastian? All we know about her is she died on February 11, 1909; her mausoleum was built in 1915. It might be interesting to know more about the woman entombed in this boxy but elegant mausoleum, but nothing else is known. Elisabeth's final resting place, which is a blend of revival styles, has polished Corinthian columns and displays an interesting interplay between smooth and rusticated stone.

LARENDON TOMB
Metairie Cemetery
New Orleans, Louisiana

General Pierre Gustave Toutant Beauregard commissioned this unique tomb for his cherished daughter, Laure Beauregard Larendon (1850–84). General Beauregard achieved immortality as the officer who ordered the first shots fired at Fort Sumter that began the Civil War. His daughter is immortalized by this one-of-a-kind tomb.

The tomb in which Laure is spending eternity with her husband and two children was built in 1885 of dark Belgian limestone. The design is Moorish, with lobed horseshoe arches and a modified dome crowned with an Eastern Orthodox cross. The somber mood of the structure is enlivened by a circular stained glass window set into one of the arches.

MASON MAUSOLEUM
Woodlawn Cemetery
Bronx, New York

Thomas F. Mason's (d. 1899) tidy little Classical Revival mausoleum is a showcase for bas-relief panels. The double doors are embellished with Victorian geometric floral designs.

The panel on the left shows an angel taking inventory of Thomas Mason's life and is inscribed with the Latin words, *Ab Initio, Ad Finem* ("from beginning to end"). The panel on the right depicts an angel with a horn, presumably Gabriel, awaiting the results of the inventory. Will he pick up his horn and signal to the heavens the imminent arrival of Thomas Mason's soul? Or . . . The panel is inscribed with the Latin phrase, *Sic Transit Gloria Mundi* ("thus passes away the glory of the world"). The phrase is from the "Service of the Pope's Enthronement." At the moment it is uttered, a handful of flax is burned to indicate the transitoriness of earthly grandeur. A similar rite is said to have been used in the triumphal processions of the Roman Republic. In other words, you can't take it with you.

LORILLARD MAUSOLEUM
Woodlawn Cemetery
Bronx, New York

The twin Ionic-columned Lorillard mausoleum, built circa 1887, nestles comfortably in a deeply shaded glen at Woodlawn cemetery. Its heavily rusticated stone walls provide a ready surface for vines and other foliage to attach themselves.

George Lyndes Lorillard (d. 1886) and other family members achieved considerable wealth as owners of the Lorillard Tobacco Company. Like many wealthy families in the latter half of the nineteenth century, they also had interests in horse racing and breeding. The Lorillard Stables were known by enthusiastic turfmen throughout the world.

Another family member, Griswald Lorillard, had a reputation as an entertainer. One year at the Tuxedo Club Ball, Griswald decided to break with the tradition of wearing white-tie formal attire and wore instead a black jacket with black satin trim. His inventive new style in men's apparel became known as the tuxedo. Griswald was one of the founders of the town Tuxedo Park in New York.

LEFEBVRE MAUSOLEUM

Metairie Cemetery
New Orleans, Louisiana

Most brick mausoleums are rather plain affairs, in which utility and economy of construction are of prime importance. Often, they are covered with stucco or similar materials to provide some character. The Lefebvre mausoleum is an exception to the rule and is truly a tribute to the bricklayer's art. All of the architectural ornament in this Classical Revival mausoleum is expressed in brick. Pediments, column capitals, dentils, engaged columns and embossed panels — all are brick. The only nonbrick forms are marble tablets calling the roll of departed family members. The Lefebvre family have been buried in the mausoleum since its construction over 100 years ago.

Although cemetery records do not indicate the designer or builder of the mausoleum, its inspiration appears to have been none other than the tomb of Cyrus the Great in ancient Persia.

SLARK AND LETCHFORD TOMBS

Cypress Grove Cemetery
New Orleans, Louisiana

—⚬—

Both of these tombs, constructed in 1868, are classified under the broad umbrella of revival styles of architecture, the Slark mausoleum leaning toward Classical Revival and the Letchford more in keeping with Gothic Revival forms. It looks as though some giant stepped on the Letchford tomb, for all that remains above ground is its steepled top. The Letchford mausoleum is reminiscent of the early Gothic Revival period also referred to as Medieval Revival. This style of architecture was popular in the mid-nineteenth century and preceded more exuberant Victorian Gothic styles.

The tombs were probably designed by Theodore Brune and erected by George Stroud. The styling is indicative of Brune's work; both men were active in the funerary arts when these two mausoleums were constructed. Both Robert Slark (d. 1868), who was in the hardware business, and the W. H. Letchford family (the Letchford tomb contains the remains of Sarah Augusta Slark, d. 1868, wife of W. H. Letchford) were wealthy New Orleaneans. Cypress Grove Cemetery, better known as the Fireman's Cemetery, was founded in 1840 by the Fireman's Charitable and Benevolent Association.

COLTON MAUSOLEUM
Mountain View Cemetery
Oakland, California

———

(*Opposite*) The Colton Mausoleum is a fine example of the eclecticism of designer Fulgenzio Seregni. A native of Milan, Seregni billed himself as a "designer of artworks of a memorial nature." He designed mausoleums all over the United States. Here in Oakland's Mountain View Cemetery, in addition to the Colton mausoleum, he designed two Gothic Revival mausoleums and numerous monuments.

For the Colton mausoleum Seregni chose a basic Greek Revival temple with Corinthian columns and pilasters, complete with twin sphinxes to guard the Colton remains. Although sphinxes and Greek Revival temples are considered pagan architectural forms, they continue to be among the most popular types of funerary architecture.

Mrs. David D. Colton had this mausoleum built for her husband following his death in 1878. Colton was legal counsel to the "Big Four" of transcontinental rail-

road fame — sometimes known as the "big four and one-half," with the addition of Colton. When Colton died, his wife tried to collect on the shares of the railroad she now owned, but the railroad gave her a very low valuation on those shares. She sued, and the resulting trial, which she did not win, nevertheless exposed the widespread corruption and political bribery exercised by the railroad.

As an expression of her grief, Colton's widow had his mausoleum built in a location that would be plainly visible from her Nob Hill residence across the bay in San Francisco.

COLTON MAUSOLEUM VIEW
Mountain View Cemetery
Oakland, California

———

(*Above*) Standing in front of the door of the Colton mausoleum and looking west toward San Francisco, the viewer can plainly see Nob Hill at the center of the photograph.

RODGERS MAUSOLEUM

Cypress Lawn Memorial Park
Colma, California

Built in 1929, the Egyptian Revival Rodgers mausoleum is a result of the "Tut Mania" that swept across the United States in the 1920s. Almost all Egyptian architecture is funerary in nature and, despite its pagan origins, became quite popular in nonsectarian cemeteries of the late nineteenth and early twentieth centuries.

Above the entrance to the tomb are vulture's wings, a symbol of protection and maternal care. Between the wings are a circular disk representing the sun and twin cobras denoting death. Two lotus-styled columns flank the battered entry, and an eternal flame crowns the tomb. A pair of marble sphinxes guard the Rodgers's remains.

Arthur Rodgers (1848–1929) was a prominent attorney and a regent of the University of California.

FLOOD MAUSOLEUM

Cypress Lawn Memorial Park
Colma, California

❧

The Flood mausoleum is a restrained but elegant example of Beaux-Arts symmetry in the form of a Greek temple. Twenty-eight Ionic, polished granite columns support the intersecting cross-gables. Although it is not documented, it is likely that Augustus J. Laver, who designed Flood's Menlo Park estate, "Linden Towers," and his San Francisco mansion, also designed his mausoleum. Well-heeled citizens like James Flood frequently employed the same architect to design their private residences and their mausoleums.

Constructed in 1889, the Flood mausoleum was originally located in the Laurel Hill Cemetery in San Francisco. In 1905, the entire mausoleum, as well as Flood's remains, was moved 10 miles south to Cypress Lawn cemetery, in Colma. The mausoleum escaped the disastrous 1906 earthquake unharmed. It remains today one of the most beautiful examples of funerary architecture in Cypress Lawn Memorial Park.

James Clair Flood (1826–89), son of Irish immigrant parents, arrived in California in 1849. He teamed up with a fellow Irishman, William O'Brien, and opened a saloon in San Francisco. The two men bought up Nevada mining claims from their saloon patrons. With some astute speculation, they soon found themselves in control of the vast Comstock Lode. Four years after quitting the saloon business, Flood was earning more than $500,000 a month. Flood established the Nevada Bank in 1875, which after his death merged with the Wells Fargo Bank.

MILLER MAUSOLEUM
West Laurel Hill Cemetery
Bala Cynwyd, Pennsylvania

The George Miller mausoleum is rare in both its architecture and history. It was designed and erected by the Harrison Granite Company in New York City in 1919 in the form of a medieval "keep." Keeps are the main towers of castles and were usually designed with sufficient space to serve as living quarters for royal or noble families in times of siege. One might think, therefore, the Miller family to be of royal lineage but such is not the case.

The Miller mausoleum is an oddity in the funerary industry: It is a "used" or, perhaps more delicately put, "previously owned" mausoleum. The mau-

soleum was originally commissioned by Adam Tindel, who bought the lot in 1919. Later that year, the mausoleum was erected, followed closely by the interment of Harris Emory Tindel. During the next few years several more Tindels were received into the mausoleum's crypts. Then, according to cemetery records, on December 7, 1928, an order was issued to transfer the bodies to another section of the cemetery and to sandblast the Tindel name off the mausoleum.

Evidently, George Miller had purchased the previously occupied mausoleum, and cemetery records indicate that on January 6, 1937, his ashes were placed in crypt #3. The next few decades saw a number of Miller family interments. The Miller mausoleum continued to be used through the 1980s.

SPOTTS MAUSOLEUM
Cavehill Cemetery
Louisville, Kentucky

(*Below*) John Baird of Philadelphia designed and erected this marble mausoleum in 1866, in an Islamic style with Classical embellishments. Baird was an innovator in the use of steam power for cutting marble. He eventually built, on the Schuylkill River, the largest establishment for the sawing and manufacture of marble in the United States.

The mausoleum was commissioned by Mrs. Spotts, the widow of Captain Harry I. Spotts, a popular Louisville steamboat captain. The Islamic/Moorish lines and the entire shape of the mausoleum (only the front is seen in the photograph), are reminiscent of a funeral barge, perhaps a nod to Captain Spott's career on the Ohio River.

BRADBURY MAUSOLEUM
Mountain View Cemetery
Oakland, California

(*Above*) The Bradbury mausoleum on Mountain View Cemetery's Millionaires Row is composed of various Egyptian (the pyramidal roof and battered entry) and Classical Revival forms (the corner pilasters), assembled in a creative manner. Angels are often used in mausoleum architecture. In the Bradbury mausoleum, the angel is right at the door. Closer inspection reveals that the angel is able to slide out of the way to allow access to visitors, both permanent and temporary. But to prevent her from moving too far, she is secured with a chain and lock. Stand on the steps of the Bradbury mausoleum and you'll be graced with heavenly views of San Francisco from this lofty perch. The mausoleum is the final resting place of Lewis L. Bradbury (1822–92), a native of Bangor, Maine, his wife, Simona, and their daughter, Rosario Bradbury Winston.

GHEENS MAUSOLEUM
Cave Hill Cemetery
Louisville, Kentucky

(*Below*) Charles W. Gheens (1837–1927) wasn't about to take any chances when it came to selecting and building his final resting spot. Gheens apparently reasoned that death could come at any moment, so he planned ahead and built his mausoleum when he was only thirty-seven years old. Gheens was engaged in a number of businesses, including wholesale groceries, cement manufacturing and real estate. He contributed to many charities and actively supported the Southern Baptist Theological Seminary.

The minutes of the Cave Hill Cemetery Board of Managers for May 7, 1874 stated: "Charles W. Gheens submitted drawings for a family vault to be erected on a lot selected for that purpose by Mr. Robert Ross, Superintendent, soliciting a permit therefore which was unanimously granted." After completing construction of his mausoleum, Charles lived for another fifty-three years, dying at the ripe old age of ninety in New Orleans.

The Gheens mausoleum is a fine example of a Gothic Revival chapel mausoleum. Miniature buildings in the shape of a church are known as aedicules.

GWIN MAUSOLEUM
Mountain View Cemetery
Oakland, California

(*Above*) The Gwin Mausoleum is one of two pyramid mausoleums in Mountain View Cemetery. Egyptian-style architecture is generally funerary, since much of the architecture of ancient Egypt was somehow connected with death and the afterlife. The obvious pagan references of the Egyptian style were bothersome to Christians, however, so tomb builders frequently added Christian symbols to their mausoleums. Sometimes a Christian angel replaced a pagan sphinx, or a crucifix or other Christian symbol was incorporated in the overall design.

The Gwin pyramid uses rusticated stone in contrast to the smooth forms of the gateway entry and base. The gateway includes pylonlike battered forms and a cavetto cornice (flared, with curve). The only deviation from the Egyptian style is the Greco-Roman pediment atop the entry.

William McKendree Gwin (1805–85), a native of Tennessee, held a number of minor federal offices during the presidencies of Jackson and Polk. In 1849, along with many other Americans, he ventured to California via the Isthmus of Panama. Within three months of his arrival, this persuasive and ambitious man became a delegate to the state constitutional convention held in Monterey, California, in September 1849. At the convention, Gwin argued successfully that California ought to be a state rather than a territory. To complete his meteoric political rise, he was elected, as was John C. Frémont, to the post of U.S. senator in December 1849, ten months before California formally became a state.

CROCKER MONUMENT

Upper Tier, Millionaires Row
Mountain View Cemetery
Oakland, California

⚬

(*Above*) Sharing the top of Mountain View Cemetery's Millionaires Row are the Merritt Mausoleum (out of view on the right, see page 30) and the Crocker Monument. The circular Crocker monument, constructed in 1888, was built in the style of a pavilion. These round "tholos" forms were inspired by temples and tombs of Greco-Roman antiquity. The smooth sides of the mausoleum are in contrast to the rusticated stone blocks forming the base of the structure.

The Crocker mausoleum was designed by New York–born architect Arthur Page Brown. Brown studied at the École des Beaux-Arts in Paris before working for the prestigious New York architectural firm of McKim, Mead and White. He moved to California in 1889. In 1893, he won the design competition for the California Building at the Chicago Columbian Exposition, then designed the famous Ferry Building in San Francisco in 1896. Brown's life was cut tragically short by a traffic accident later in 1896.

Following Charles Crocker's death in 1888, his wife Mary commissioned Brown, then living in New York, to build this tomb for her husband. Charles Crocker was one of the "Big Four" who built the western portion of the transcontinental railroad. Ironically, like Brown, Crocker was also killed in a carriage accident. Curiously, since the monument is solid granite, none of the Crockers are entombed inside. Nevertheless, cemetery records indicate that somewhere around the monument lie the mortal remains of Charles Crocker, his wife Mary, their son George and George's wife Emma.

ROMANESQUE ROW

Mountain View Cemetery
Oakland, California

⚬

(*Pages 68–69*) This row of Romanesque Revival mausoleums, nestling on the hillside, is the eternal home of a number of San Francisco's founding fathers. Although at first glance the mausoleums all appear the same, there are subtle differences. The corner turrets, rusticated masonry and round arches are characteristics of Richardsonian Romanesque architecture of the late nineteenth century.

CORNELIUS SMITH MAUSOLEUM

Oakwood Cemetery
Syracuse, New York

The mausoleum of Lyman Cornelius Smith (1850–1910) is one of the grandest in a cemetery full of grand mausoleums. It is designed in a classically elegant Beaux-Arts style, complete with four delicately carved Corinthian columns projecting from the facade, and a number of squared-off, engaged Corinthian columns ringing the building. Inside the mausoleum is a well-secured Tiffany stained glass window sandwiched between two pieces of 1-inch-thick plate glass.

Lyman Cornelius Smith was an industrialist and capitalist who possessed a vast empire of business holdings, including banks, steamship companies, shipbuilding companies, steel mills and railroads. His later years were devoted to developing his best-known product, the typewriter. Along with his brothers, he manufactured the Smith-Premier typewriter and the L. C. Smith and Brothers typewriters.

BURNET MAUSOLEUM

Spring Grove Cemetery
Cincinnati, Ohio

The facade of this imported Italian marble vault is typical of the exuberant decoration and form found in the baroque style of architecture. Erected in 1865, it was designed by Cincinnati architect Charles Rule for the Burnet family. Rule's design includes twin cherubs leaning against an urn over the entry. Two other urns are topped by the flame of life.

Judge Jacob Burnet originally had a vault in Cincinnati's Presbyterian Churchyard, but fearing urban development, he gave up his churchyard plot and purchased a plot at Spring Grove. He died in 1853 and was buried in the Spring Grove plot. However, his wife had her own ideas about where she wanted to spend eternity and had this mausoleum built to Charles Rule's design. In 1865, the judge's remains were disinterred and placed in the newly completed Burnet mausoleum, which he shares with his wife and son.

SMITH MAUSOLEUM

Mountain View Cemetery
Oakland, California

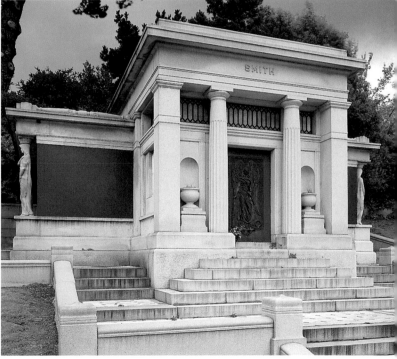

The crisp lines of the Smith mausoleum, located on Mountain View Cemetery's Millionaires Row are reminiscent of Romantic Classicism. The basic form of the mausoleum is Greco-Roman, with modified Doric columns and blue and white stained glass clerestory windows. Female figures abound, as four caryatids flank the building, and a mournful, bronze bas-relief angel graces the door. The stepped and terraced base integrates the building with its site. This architectural concept was first seen in the tomb complex of Zoser, in Egypt, in 2600 B.C.

Francis Marion "Borax" Smith was a Nevada miner. He became a partner of William Coleman in 1880, and they developed a rich borax claim in Death Valley, California. The method they developed for transporting the raw borax out of Death Valley to the nearest rail head, 165 miles distant, soon became a household name — Twenty-Mule Team Borax.

WHITE MAUSOLEUM
Mount Auburn Cemetery
Cambridge, Massachusetts

Ralph H. White's last resting place, designed by architect Willard Sears, looks much like the town hall of a thriving metropolis. The massive cupola, resembling a bell tower without the bell, is supported by twelve Ionic columns. Circling the top of the dome is a ring of garlands. Punctuating Ralph White's memorial in Classical Revival architecture is an eternal flame, frozen in granite, complete with lightning rod. R. H. White owned a large department store that was a Boston-area landmark.

MANGER MAUSOLEUM
Woodlawn Cemetery
Bronx, New York

(*Opposite*) Apparently, someone got hold of a Classical Revival granite catalog and ordered one of everything, or two, three or four of everything. Cemetery records indicate the Manger mausoleum was built around 1927, making it one of the last hurrahs of mausoleum construction. The Great Depression hit and effectively ended the golden age of mausoleum construction. Hallmarks of the Manger mausoleum are use of both Ionic and Corinthian columns, high relief garlands under the dome, a Madonna and Child sculpture over the portico and eternal flames bending in the breeze.

Cemetery records are devoid of information about Julius Manger, except that he died on March 28, 1937. Other records, however, indicate that Julius Manger was connected with the Pharmacological Institute in Würzburg, Germany, where he performed tests on the accuracy of an ancient Egyptian pregnancy test. In ancient Egypt, a woman could determine if she was pregnant by urinating daily on a bag of barley and wheat. If barley grew, she would have a girl; if wheat grew, she would have a boy; if nothing grew, she wasn't pregnant. According to Manger's 1933 report, he conducted a series of tests and found that the urine of pregnant women who gave birth to boys promotes the growth of wheat, and the urine of women who gave birth to girls promoted the growth of barley — fascinating!

WINTER MAUSOLEUM
Allegheny Cemetery
Pittsburgh, Pennsylvania

The Winter mausoleum, built in 1930, appears to be an exact duplicate of the Woolworth mausoleum, built in 1920 and located in Woodlawn Cemetery in the Bronx. Architect John Russell Pope designed the Woolworth mausoleum. Judging from the similarity between the two mausoleums, Pope appears to have been involved with, or at least to have consulted on, the Winter mausoleum. With their clean lines and stylized ornaments, both mausoleums are a departure from older forms of Egyptian Revival architecture. Their rather buxom sphinxes are derived from Greek architecture, where sphinxes were always female, but other details, such as the vulture wings, cobras and sun are all taken from ancient Egyptian architecture.

Emil Winter (1857–1935) was president of the Workingmen's Savings Bank and Trust Company in Pittsburgh and was also head of a number of metal production companies. He had a large overseas plant in Austria for processing manganese ore and was one the founders of the Pittsburgh Steel Company. As grand as his mausoleum is, it is overshadowed by Lyndhurst, his opulent home in the Squirrel Hill area of Pittsburgh.

WINTER MAUSOLEUM DOOR
Allegheny Cemetery
Pittsburgh, Pennsylvania

The bronze door of the Winter mausoleum is a treasure trove of Egyptian symbols, the most widely known being the *ankh* held by both male figures. The *ankh* is a symbol of immortaliy, often depicted in the hands of Egyptian gods. It combines two Egyptian symbols, the T cross, or *tau* (symbol of Osiris), and the oval (symbol of Isis).

At the top of the door are twin vultures, representing maternal care.

WOOLWORTH MAUSOLEUM

Woodlawn Cemetery
Bronx, New York

The Woolworth mausoleum predates the Winter mausoleum, which appears to be an exact duplicate. Architect John Russell Pope designed this mausoleum in 1920. Pope later designed the Jefferson Memorial in Washington, D.C.

F. W. Woolworth (1852–1919) developed a sales formula based on attractive displays and reasonable fixed prices. He cunningly realized that pricing articles for sale in increments of 5 and 10 cents, the most commonly used coins at the time, encouraged sales. Woolworth found that such business practices encouraged impulse buying and generated increased sales and revenues. By the time of his death, there were over 1,000 of his "five and dime" stores.

Poor F. W. took his own frugality, however, a little too far: He died of septic poisoning because he didn't want to pay to see a dentist.

Woolworth's adventurous architectural tastes were not limited to his eternal home. He also built an architectural gem of a building to house his corporate offices in lower Manhattan. He and his architect had a sense of style and humor. Gargoyles incorporated into the decorative elements of the interior are cast with faces of individuals instrumental in the building's construction. Perhaps the incredibly buxom sphinxes on his mausoleum reflect his sense of humor — or maybe wishful thinking.

Also entombed in the Woolworth mausoleum is Woolworth's granddaughter, the much married socialite Barbara Hutton (1912–79).

REPLICA MAUSOLEUMS

Interpretations of Classical Architecture

To echo the old saying, "If it works, don't fix it," these mausoleums are copies and interpretations of enduring historic structures. Sometimes architects based their mausoleum designs on classic structures, such as the Parthenon, Pantheon and Tower of the Winds. Of these ancient architectural wonders, the Parthenon is probably most copied in mausoleum architecture. Mausoleum architects also found inspiration in less well-known structures, such as the Kiosk of Trajan at the Temple of Isis on the Island of Philae, Egypt. The beautiful Kiosk of Trajan was the model for Jules Bache's mausoleum in Woodlawn Cemetery in the Bronx.

FLEISCHMAN MAUSOLEUM

Spring Grove Cemetery
Cincinnati, Ohio

(*Opposite*) William Salway, the superintendent of Spring Grove Cemetery, designed this miniaturized, peristyled Doric temple, reminiscent of the Parthenon, for the Fleischman family in 1913. Salway, who was trained as an engineer and landscape gardener in England, had taken the job of superintendent in 1883 following the death of former superintendent Adolph Strauch. Strauch came to Spring Grove in 1854 and introduced the "Landscape Lawn Plan" of cemetery design, establishing Spring Grove as one of the most attractively

There are mausoleaums that are full-scale copies of historic buildings, such as the Belmont mausoleum, also in Woodlawn Cemetery in the Bronx. It is a replica of Leonardo da Vinci's burial place, the Chapel of St. Hubert in France. A more personal mausoleum is the Egan family tomb in Metairie Cemetery in New Orleans. It is identical to a ruined chapel on the family's estate in Ireland.

Whether Greek Revival, Classical Revival, Egyptian Revival or Gothic Revival, all the original structures have stood the test of time. They are copied time and again in mausoleums and other more conventional buildings all over the world.

landscaped cemeteries in the country, a distinction that remains to this day.

In designing the Fleischman mausoleum, Salway combined Neoclassical architecture with Naturalism to to create a rustic but ordered effect. The combination of the white temple (inspired by the 1893 World's Columbian Exhibition in Chicago), the plantings and the lake creates a picture much like the famous English garden at Stourhead.

W. H. Harrison, president of the Harrison Granite company in New York, erected the mausoleum using 5,000 cubic feet of Barre (Vermont) granite. The walls are 18 inches thick. Recessed into one of them is a well-secured stained glass window depicting the Three Fates.

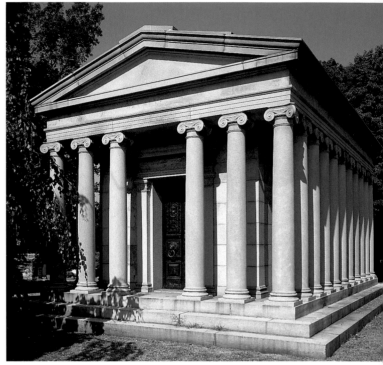

BYERS MAUSOLEUM

Allegheny Cemetery
Pittsburgh, Pennsylvania

———

(*Left*) The multicolumned Byers mausoleum, built in 1902, is a perfect small-scale Grecian Doric temple. The only break in the symmetry of the columns is the gap in front of the doorway. This gap is just wide enough to allow for the passage of a funeral procession carrying a casket into the mausoleum.

Alexander McBurney Byers (1827–1900) was in iron making for his entire adult life. He became a blast furnace superintendent at age 16, and in 1864 was a founder of the iron and pipe making firm Graff, Byers & Co., which became A.M. Byers & Co. in 1886. His firm was noted for the Aston-Byers process that used Bessemer converters to make wrought iron pipe.

GOULD MAUSOLEUM

Woodlawn Cemetery
Bronx, New York

———

(*Right*) Architect H. Q. French of New York designed this Ionic peripteral temple mausoleum, reminiscent of the Parthenon, for Jay Gould (1834–92), the man who personified the term "robber baron." French was the designer of a number of elegant tombs, most of them in the Classical Revival style. Unfortunately, little is known about French's life, but he has left behind a legacy of beautiful architecture. Adding to the beauty of the Gould mausoleum is a huge weeping birch tree, which was designated one of the "113 Great Trees in New York City" in 1985.

A number of members of the Gould family are entombed in the mausoleum, including Gould's wife, Helen, who died in 1889, and a number of their children. All of the caskets are in wall crypts. Interestingly, Jay Gould's crypt is soldered closed. Accounts of the day suggest that some of Gould's enemies on Wall Street had the casket sealed so there was no way he could ever show up to wreak havoc again. Apparently, too, the Gould family didn't want a repeat of an incident that occurred in 1876, when the body of another millionaire, A. J. Stewart, was stolen from St. Mark's Cemetery in Manhattan, and his remains held for ransom. An undisclosed amount of money was paid by Mrs. Stewart for the return of what was presumed to be her husband (embalming wasn't an exact science in the 1870s).

The *London Times* obituary summed up Gould's life in declaring, "All honor to the greatest money maker of any age or clime. He was less a man than a machine for churning wealth. Napoleon's combinations were never vaster. . . . It will be impossible to explain one phase of civilization without a frequent mention of his name."

BINDLEY MAUSOLEUM
Allegheny Cemetery
Pittsburgh, Pennsylvania

The Bindley mausoleum, built in 1907, is a replica or interpretation of the Pantheon. The original Pantheon, built in Rome c. A.D. 118–128 during the reign of the Emperor Hadrian, heralded a new era in Western architecture in which spatial volume became more important than physical structure. The Pantheon and the Bindley mausoleum are both domed round drums fronted by traditional temple porticoes and pediments.

The proportions of the Pantheon (the original in Rome) were carefully calculated so that if the curve of the inside of the dome were extended downward, it would "kiss" the floor, creating a perfect sphere within the volume of the building. This was a symbolic reference to the temple's dedication to all ("pan") the gods ("theos").

The Bindley Pantheon, with its softly rusticated granite block walls, Corinthian columns and sky-lit dome, is a study in subtle elegance. The Bindleys were financiers who owned a number of businesses. John Bindley was one of the original corporators of Allegheny Cemetery.

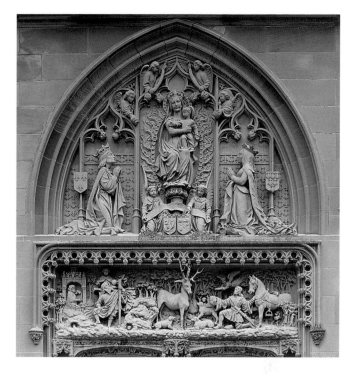

BELMONT MAUSOLEUM

Woodlawn Cemetery
Bronx, New York

〰

(*Opposite*) The Belmont mausoleum is a full-scale replica of the Chapel of St. Hubert in the Queen's section of the Chateau d'Amboise in France's famed Loire valley. This chapel was designed by Leonardo da Vinci in the "Gothic Flamboyant" style in the early 1500s. Da Vinci spent the last three years of his life in the village of Amboise as a guest of King Francis I. Upon his death in 1519, da Vinci's remains were placed in a sarcophagus in the chapel he designed. Above the doorway is a relief depicting St. Hubert, St. Christopher and an array of other religious figures.

Oliver Hazard Perry Belmont (1858–1908), who rests beneath the protruding gargoyles of his mausoleum, was hardly a religious man. O. H. P. Belmont's great love was horses. He was the founder of the Belmont Raceway. After O. H. P. died following an attack of appendicitis, his wife, Alva Vanderbilt Belmont (she was previously married to William K. Vanderbilt), used her fortune to support the growing suffragist movement. Alva lived a long life and, after her death in Paris in 1933, her remains were interred in the Belmont mausoleum. With Alva was buried the suffragette banner she carried, inscribed with the words, "Failure is impossible." The banner hangs inside the mausoleum.

BELMONT MAUSOLEUM DETAIL

Woodlawn Cemetery
Bronx, New York

〰

(*Above*) Architect R. H. Hunt, in designing the relief panels above the entry of the Belmont mausoleum, made very few changes from the originals on the Chapel of St. Hubert in Amboise, France. The central figure in the lintel is a stag with what looks like a crucifix growing from its head. (The crucifix is actually supposed to be wedged in its antlers.) The image represents the stag that caused St. Hubert to convert to Christianity. St. Hubert, (patron saint of the hunt) is also present on the panel, as are St. Christopher, St. Anthony, dogs, angels, cherubs and various woodland creatures. The tympanum's central figures are the Madonna and Child, flanked by kneeling figures of Charles VIII of France and his queen, Anne of Brittany.

R. H. Hunt and his father, Richard Morris Hunt, were partners in an architectural firm that specialized in designing residences for the rich and famous. Richard Morris Hunt designed residences for Alva Belmont when she was a Vanderbilt; R. H. Hunt designed this mausoleum for her when she was a Belmont. She may have switched husbands, but she knew a good architectural firm when she found one.

EGAN TOMB
Metairie Cemetery
New Orleans, Louisiana

(*Left*) It appears the Egan family tomb has fallen into disrepair and is gently crumbling into the earth; in fact, the tomb is in quite good repair and should stand for many years to come. The Egan tomb, built in the late 1800s of Tennessee marble, is one of the most unique and creative replica tombs in the world. Often referred to as "the ruined castle," its design is taken from a little chapel on the family's estate in Ireland that had been burned and vandalized and lay in ruins.

The design has been attributed to Pierre Casse, who skillfully carved the marble to make it appear chipped, cracked and broken. To complete the illusion, the slab containing the names of the fallen Egans (on the floor of the tomb, covering the underground crypts) also appears to be cracked. Perhaps the tomb is a representation of life cut short: It contains the remains of two Egan youths who died in the Civil War, twenty-four-year-old Henry Egan, who was killed at Amelia Springs, Virginia, on April 6, 1865, and twenty-four-year-old Yelverton Egan, who was killed at the Battle of Sharpsburg (Antietam) on September 17, 1863.

The inscription above the Gothic arch, *Sic itur ad astra* ("thus is accomplished the journey to the stars"), is from Virgil's *Aeneid*, Book IX, line 641, written in 19 B.C.

VACCARO MAUSOLEUM
Metairie Cemetery
New Orleans, Louisiana

(*Opposite, left*) Three Vaccaros (Joseph, Felix and Luca) have mausoleums on Metairie Avenue, but the Luca Vaccaro mausoleum, built in 1925, is the most interesting. It is a personal interpretation of the Tower of the Winds in Athens. The Tower of the Winds, c. 40 B.C., an octagonal building designed by Andronicus Cyrrus, served as a weather guide and water clock. On each of the eight frieze panels were carvings of personified winds. The structure in Athens had three porticoes (one round and two square) attached to its sides. For the Vaccaro mausoleum, sculptor Theodore Bottinelli carved some frieze panels as they appear in the Athenian temple, but for other panels he chose more funerary themes, such as a young man holding a torch and an hourglass and a young woman playing a harp.

BERWIND MAUSOLEUM

West Laurel Hill Cemetery
Bala Cynwyd, Pennsylvania

(*Above, right*) The Berwind mausoleum is a remarkably authentic adaptation of the Tower of the Winds in Athens. The only difference is the Berwind mausoleum is minus the porticoes found on the original. The mausoleum sports eight frieze panels, each carved to represent one of the personified winds. In the center of the photograph, above the entry, is Kaikias, the Northeast Wind; on the right, holding an oil lamp, is Boreas, the North Wind; and on the left, holding a spray of flowers, is Apeliotes, the East Wind. The Tower of the Winds in Athens was designed to measure time by means of a water clock inside the structure and a sundial mounted on the outside. The Berwind mausoleum, by contrast, houses only Berwinds.

The Berwind mausoleum was designed by architect Horace Trumbauer, who also designed the Berwind family's estate, The Elms, in Newport, Rhode Island. Horace Trumbauer (1876–1938) is buried in a sarcophagus in another section of West Laurel Hill. Trumbauer was a noted architect of the early twentieth century. His buildings in Philadelphia, New York, Newport, Washington, D.C., and Grosse Point, Michigan, were frequently modeled after European structures and designs.

Edward J. Berwind (1848–1936) is best described as a capitalist whose fortune was made in the coal business. Like most capitalists, he had a number of diversified businesses. When he died in 1936, his estate was valued at $31 million.

BACHE MAUSOLEUM
Woodlawn Cemetery
Bronx, New York

(*Opposite*) Woodlawn Cemetery in the Bronx is the final address of some of America's wealthiest citizens. Jules Bache (1861–1944) rests among the many "robber barons" and millionaires he lived with. Bache made his living as a stockbroker and was a longtime collector and patron of the arts, donating a number of Goyas and Rembrandts to the Metropolitan Museum of Art. Bache's tomb reflects his interest in the arts. He chose as his mausoleum a replica of the elegant Kiosk of Trajan or "pharaoh's bed" at the Temple of Isis on the island of Philae on the Nile River. Isis was one of humanity's most worshipped goddesses. The ancient scholar Apuleius gave her a voice in *The Golden Ass*: "At my will the planets of the sky, the wholesome winds of the sea, and the lamentable silences of Hell are disposed; my name, my divinity is adored throughout the world." Perhaps Bache felt inspired by Isis's teachings.

Bache's kiosk was designed by architect John Russell Pope, who later designed the Jefferson Memorial in Washington, D.C. The sheer size of the Bache mausoleum makes it one of a kind. The hallmarks of the Bache mausoleum are its massive columns capped with abstractions of lotus blossoms (signifying the unfolding creative universe) and the open-roof design. Replica mausoleums are common in cemeteries; interpretations of the Parthenon, Pantheon, Gothic chapels and cathedral replicas may be seen in most large metropolitan cemeteries.

KIOSK OF TRAJAN
Island of Philae, Egypt

(*Below*) This swan song of Egyptian architecture was never fully completed. The Temple of Isis, the goddess of salvation, was Egypt's last functioning temple and housed the last priests able to read and write hieroglyphics in the demotic style.

The entire Temple of Isis of Philae, including the Kiosk of Trajan, was disassembled and transported to higher ground from 1972 to 1980, when rising waters from the Aswan Dam threatened to engulf the island; thus, this beautiful architecture was saved from total destruction.

This illustration is from the book *Description de l'Égypte*, commissioned by Napoleon in 1802 and completed over twenty years by 400 copper-engravers. It was finally published in 1822.

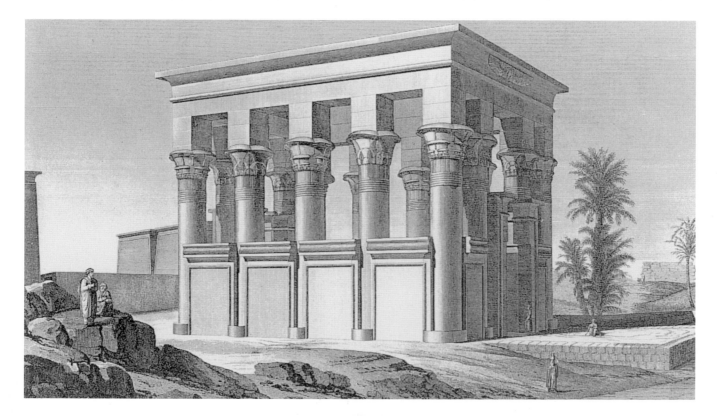

DEXTER CHAPEL/MAUSOLEUM

Spring Grove Cemetery
Cincinnati, Ohio

———

(*Below, left*) It took four years (from 1865 to 1869) for Cincinnati architect James Keyes Wilson to design this Gothic Revival combination chapel and mausoleum for the Dexter brothers — the chapel is above and the crypts are below. The Dexter brothers wanted a structure reminiscent of the Sainte-Chapelle in Paris; however, Wilson may also have been inspired by Chichester Cathedral in England. With its flamboyant design and massive flying buttresses, this is considered one of the most beautiful buildings in the Cincinnati area.

The $100,000 cost of the mausoleum was extravagant for its time, but it has long been a centerpiece of Spring Grove Cemetery. The mausoleum has unfortunately been plagued by structural problems almost from the beginning. Its sandstone walls were once covered with ivy, which contributed to its decay. Many of the turrets, crockets and pinnacles have deteriorated and fallen to the ground. Despite periodic attempts at restoration, the structure may have to be torn down.

FLYING BUTTRESSES/ DEXTER MAUSOLEUM

Spring Grove Cemetery
Cincinnati, Ohio

———

(*Below, right*) When it was finished in 1869, the Dexter mausoleum boasted the only flying buttresses in the Cincinnati area. These architectural wonders are fashioned to give buildings extra strength by transmitting the thrust of a vault or roof from the upper part of a wall to an outer support, known as a buttress. When the buttresses are open, as seen in the Dexter mausoleum, rather than solid, they are known as flying buttresses.

McCAN MAUSOLEUM

Metairie Cemetery
New Orleans, Louisiana

The David McCan mausoleum, with its Gothic Revival form and strong verticality, is reminiscent of the Albert Memorial in London's South Kensington district. The death of Queen Victoria's consort, Albert, in 1861 was one of the major factors in popularizing the funerary arts. One of Queen Victoria's first memorials to Prince Albert was the Albert Memorial.

Albert died at age 42, following a bout of typhoid fever. According to the queen, their son Edward, prince of Wales, brought on Albert's illness. It seems Edward's unseemly behavior caused Albert to explode in a fit of rage, resulting in irreparable damage to his health. So great was Edward's sin in Victoria's mind that she never forgave her son for his behavior.

Albert's death threw the queen into a mourning frenzy. She wore only black clothing for the remaining forty years of her life; went to bed every night clutching Albert's nightshirt; kept a portrait of him on the pillow next to her; and memorialized him ad infinitum. She had numerous monuments and buildings constructed in his memory. One of the results of Victoria's immense influence on culture — an entire era was named for her — was that memorials became highly fashionable.

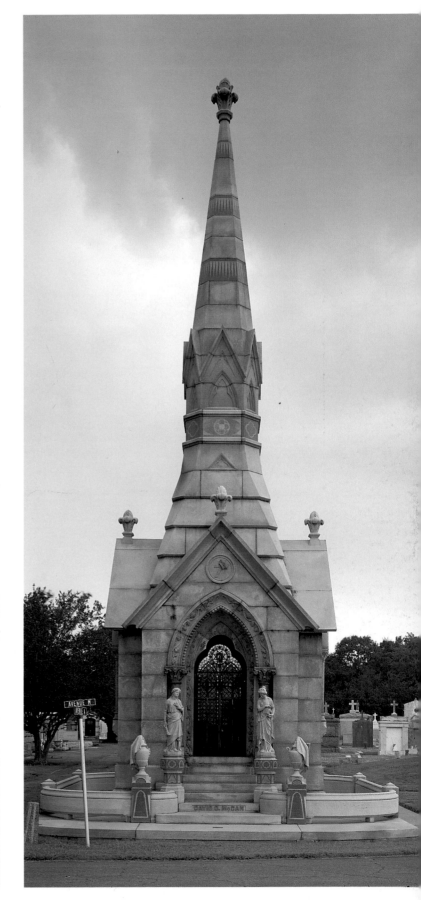

COGSWELL

UNIQUELY FUNERARY

Creativity in the Funerary Arts

Not all architecture fits into the customary architectural styles. We've therefore invented a name for these architectural deviants, "uniquely funerary." Here we see architects and designers at their creative and playful best.

Frank Lloyd Wright once mused about how delightful it was to design mausoleums, since he didn't have to worry about windows that opened, how spaces flowed together or where to run utilities, such as plumbing and electrical systems.

Indeed, mausoleums are a triumph of form over function. Architects often blended styles and sometimes created styles of their own. Nonarchitects, such as John

Blocher, who had taken up sculpting as a pastime after his retirement as a shoe manufacturer, created a mausoleum based on his own personal vision (see page 98).

The closest type of architecture to which these whimsical structures can be compared are the Victorian "follies." A folly is defined by Penguin's *Dictionary of Architecture* as "a costly, but useless structure built to satisfy the whim of some eccentric and thought to show his folly . . . "

We're not about to take on the task of defining what is useful or useless, but we are sure that many of these uniquely funerary mausoleums will amaze and delight you.

COGSWELL MONUMENT

Mountain View Cemetery
Oakland, California

(*Opposite*) The Cogswell monument is a 70-foot granite obelisk crowned with a 10-inch rose crystal star and surrounded by curious carved stone sculptures. The pieces comprising the monument were carved on the East Coast, then loaded on thirty-eight freight cars for shipment to California. Records state that the 329-ton shipment was the "heaviest shipment ever made at one time across the country." After arriving at the terminus of the railroad in Oakland, the 30-ton obelisk was placed on a special wagon shipped from the East. Try as they might, twenty-four horses couldn't get the wagon to budge. Eventually, a combination of house-moving equipment and a traction engine inched the obelisk up Cemetery Avenue to the Cogswell plot. After all the pieces arrived

at the site, crews of workmen took on the task of assembling the monument.

Henry Daniel Cogswell (1820–1900) studied and practiced dentistry in Providence, Rhode Island, until his office was destroyed in a fire. Then, in 1849, he set sail for California. He sold goods in California's Mother Lode mining region but soon returned to San Francisco to set up another dental practice. In 1851 his dental office again fell victim, this time to one of San Francisco's many fires.

Cogswell eventually made a fortune as a land speculator, founded Cogswell Dental College and Cogswell Polytechnic Institute and donated considerable funds to the University of California. Cogswell was an ardent foe of demon rum, so he erected a number of water fountains across the United States. These fountains featured a bronze statue of a man who looked amazingly like Cogswell. Note the four figures flanking the obelisk: Faith, Hope, Charity and Temperance.

CROUSE MAUSOLEUM
Oakwood Cemetery
Syracuse, New York

Architect H. Q. French of New York designed this mausoleum in 1884 for John Crouse (1802–91). It is in a style that can only be described as "uniquely funerary." The main body of the Crouse tomb appears to be Romanesque Revival or "English Gothic," as it was known at the time, but certain details, such as the pistonlike columns, suggest the influence of Frank Furness. (Furness was a Philadelphia architect noted for his highly personal style.) Crouse wanted to make sure he knew what he was getting, when it came to his eternal home, so he had it built in anticipation of his death (which would occur seven years after the completion of the mausoleum), rather than have some relative attend to its construction after his death.

Crouse's eccentricities did not end with the construction of his final resting spot. Shortly after its completion, Crouse got it into his head that there should be a large granite boulder beside the mausoleum; he located a suitable one in a field 9 miles from his mausoleum. Unable to find anyone in Syracuse who could move the giant boulder, he took a trip to Barre, Vermont, to see legendary granite-mover Fayette "Fay" Cutler. Cutler agreed to do the job, and for weeks local newspapers reported on the daily progress of the 10′ x 12′ 175-ton pink granite boulder. The ivy-covered rock rests across from the mausoleum. As if that weren't enough, a single block of gray granite forms the pathway to the mausoleum. This 35-foot long, 5-foot wide and 10-inch thick stone weighs 35 tons.

John Crouse was an industrialist; known as the wealthiest man in Syracuse, he acquired the bulk of his wealth in the wholesale grocery business.

WIETING MAUSOLEUM
Oakwood Cemetery
Syracuse, New York

The jury is still out on what the architect/builder was thinking when designing the Wieting mausoleum in 1880. Some say it resembles an East Indian, Tibetan or Chinese stupa. Stupas were most frequently associated with Buddhist culture in those countries. The conical shape of stupas reflects the Buddhist belief that one proceeds in an ascending process toward unification with the divine. Indeed, in China, stupas are often used to surmount tombstones and burial chambers.

Dr. John M. Wieting (1817–88), a medical doctor, made his fortune in real estate but achieved fame as a lecturer. He discoursed on physiology and hygiene all over the world, using something known as the "apparatus" (apparently a contraption using a mannequin with removable parts). He was frequently compared to Mark Twain in his ability to hold an audience's attention.

Wieting also had a great love for the arts. He built the Wieting Opera House in Syracuse, which he and his descendants have rebuilt four times (in 1851, 1856, 1881 and 1897), following disastrous fires.

In 1878 Dr. Wieting and his wife embarked on a world tour, traveling to Japan, Singapore, Ceylon, India and Egypt. It is likely that these travels influenced the design of their mausoleum, built soon after Wieting returned from the Orient.

DUNLOP MAUSOLEUM

Woodlawn Cemetery
Bronx, New York

(*Left*) It looks as if Dr. Clark W. Dunlop opened up a mausoleum catalog and ordered one of everything. Columns, friezes, stained glass, busts of the doctor and his wife, mosaic tile, a cupola, a bronze door decorated with turned down torches — even a porchlike addition on the back — adorn the Dunlop mausoleum. The mausoleum appears to be Byzantine Revival in origin, but a number of other influences make appearances. In accordance with Dr. Dunlop's will, his pet parrot is also interred in the mausoleum! The good doctor pays homage to his feathered friend, as can be seen on the "plinth" of the building, carved to resemble parrots' feet.

In back of the Dunlop mausoleum, peeking through the foliage, is the Classical Revival mausoleum of financier/robber baron Jay Gould.

FOSTER TOMB

Woodlawn Cemetery
Bronx, New York

(*Right*) William F. Foster's (d. 1895) final resting place was built around 1899. The Tuscan columns, dentils and cupola are Classical Revival. The structure takes the form of a canopy tomb rather than a mausoleum, although its sheer size prompts its classification among mausoleums. In the simplest sense, canopy tombs are tentlike structures that shelter a sarcophagus. These constructions, usually composed of columns or pillars supporting a dome, are open-air affairs and, unlike mausoleums, have no doors restricting entry.

Canopies may be seen in a variety of different ancient architectural monuments. They didn't become part of the European and American architectural repertory until the eighteenth century, when architects began using them for garden pavilions. The decorative potential of these canopied pavilions and kiosks was soon exploited by designers of funerary monuments. They are often seen surmounting a grave or small monument or sheltering a sarcophagus.

CRISTOFORO COLOMBO SOCIETY TOMB

Metairie Cemetery
New Orleans, Louisiana

(*Below*) Perched atop the Società Cristoforo Colombo tomb, a life-size statue of the great Italian navigator Christopher Columbus points toward the New World. In the centuries to come, many Italians followed him to America, but not all achieved his status. Many of these Italians, and immigrants of other nationalities as well, formed fraternal or benevolent societies patterned after American organizations such as the Elks and the Masons. Such societies, besides being places to gather and talk, contracted with doctors and hospitals to provide access to basic medical care. The majority of the societies also provided burial places at modest cost.

By their nature, society tombs had a limited amount of space, so one's stay in the tomb was a temporary affair. After an appropriate duration, the deceased's bones were scooped up and stacked like so much cordwood; in some instances, bones would be wrapped in a lead sheet, sealed and then stacked up. Sometimes these bone warehouses, known as ossuaries, were part of the tomb; sometimes they were off-site.

There are only a few active society tombs in New Orleans today. The Cristoforo Colombo Society is no longer active, and this tomb has been refurbished and converted into a community mausoleum, whose occupants are now guaranteed permanent residence.

ITALIAN BENEVOLENT SOCIETY TOMB

St. Louis Cemetery No. 1
New Orleans, Louisiana

(*Above*) Of all the tombs in St. Louis Cemetery No. 1, the New Orleans Italian Mutual Benevolent Society's marble masterpiece is the shining star. In 1857, architect Pietro Gualdi (his name is inscribed below the word "Italia") designed this tomb, which for all the world looks like a fancy chest of drawers. Its twenty-four vaults were for the temporary use of the society's members, whose stay would generally last for a year or so before the bones would be scooped up and placed in a receptacle in the tomb's basement. The $40,000 cost of the tomb had to be shared among the society's members; it was understood that anyone's stay would be brief before joining the bones of his or her fellows.

The tomb is a fine example of the fanciful nature of the baroque style of architecture, which fittingly had its roots in Italy. Baroque architecture is characterized by exuberant decoration, sweeping, curvaceous forms and an almost playful delight in composition, all of which are evident in this society tomb. The tomb includes three elegantly carved marble statues of female figures — one holding a cross surmounting the top, one in a niche above "Italia" and another, out of view in a niche on the left, representing Charity.

MATTHEWS MAUSOLEUM/ CATAFALQUE
Green-Wood Cemetery
Brooklyn, New York

(*Left*) Despite the fact that noted art critic Effie Brower found it "depraved," the Matthews monument won an award for mortuary art in 1870. The Matthews monument is in the form of a catafalque or *castra doloris*, a type of tomb usually reserved for royalty. Catafalques are generally quite elaborate, full of symbolism and include depictions of key events of the departed's life.

John Matthews (1808–70), was known as the "soda fountain king" for his popularization of the soda fountain. By the time he died, he owned over 500 soda fountains. On his catafalque are the faces of his daughters (in the gables) and his wife (seated above him). Prostrate and almost melting into his sarcophagus, Matthews looks up at reliefs carved into the column capitals which depict events in his life — leaving England for America, pondering the idea of soda water and finally being crowned for his achievements.

MATTHEWS CATAFALQUE DETAIL
Green-Wood Cemetery
Brooklyn, New York

(*Below*) A winged gargoyle clutches his head, perhaps annoyed by the bears, squirrels, deer, lizards and other woodland creatures scurrying above him. The Matthews catafalque is a marvelous depiction of the events of John Matthews's life, incorporating representations of the things he loved.

PIERREPONT CATAFALQUE

Green-Wood Cemetery
Brooklyn, New York

This Gothic Revival catafalque, carved out of sand-stone, is the last resting place for a number of members of the Henry Evelyn Pierrepont family. Henry Pierrepont was the son of a wealthy Brooklyn landowner and gin distiller. In 1835, Henry laid out the streets for the newly incorporated city of Brooklyn. His design included eleven parks and land set aside for the development of a cemetery to be modeled after Père Lachaise Cemetery, in Paris.

As things evolved, Green-Wood Cemetery, which was dedicated on April 11, 1838, was modeled after Cambridge's Mount Auburn Cemetery (which was itself modeled after Père Lachaise). During the

decade after its dedication, additional land was purchased until Green-Wood reached its present size of 478 acres, three times that of Mount Auburn. In 1849, noted landscape architect A. J. Downing proclaimed, "Judging from the crowds of people in carriages and on foot I found constantly thronging Green-Wood and Mount Auburn, I think it is plain enough how much our citizens of all classes would enjoy public parks on a similar scale." It was, in fact, the popularity of Green-Wood Cemetery that led to the establishment of New York City's Central Park in 1856.

The design of the Pierrepont catafalque has been attributed to Richard Upjohn and his son, Richard Mitchell Upjohn. Pierrepont had also commissioned the father/son team to design the Gothic Revival entrance to Green-Wood cemetery.

RYERSON MAUSOLEUM

Graceland Cemetery
Chicago, Illinois

(*Above*) In 1887, when architect Louis Sullivan was thirty-one years old, he designed the polished, black granite Ryerson mausoleum. During the 1880s Sullivan's firm, Adler and Sullivan, built four office buildings for Martin Ryerson. When he died, his son, Martin A. Ryerson, commissioned Sullivan to design this mausoleum. Sullivan's creation is an artful blending of two Egyptian burial monuments — a pyramid, which crowns the top of the mausoleum, and a mastaba, a forerunner of the pyramid, which forms the bottom section.

Martin Ryerson (1818–87) left his New Jersey home and got as far as the wilds of Michigan, where he became a fur trader, then a general store clerk and finally a sawmill owner. Around 1850 Ryerson opened an office in Chicago for his booming lumber business. Over the next twenty years Chicago became the distribution center for the lumber trade. Ryerson became a wealthy man, first in the lumber business, then by investing in real estate and office buildings.

RYERSON MAUSOLEUM DETAIL

Graceland Cemetery
Chicago, Illinois

The finely detailed ornamentation on the gate and lock, seen here in the delicately sculpted leaves, contrasts with the strong geometric form of the mausoleum. These are features of the "Sullivanesque" style.

MOORHEAD MAUSOLEUM

Allegheny Cemetery
Pittsburgh, Pennsylvania

The Moorhead mausoleum's architecture is uniquely funerary. It is unlikely that this type of architectural mishmash would be found anywhere but in a cemetery. The mausoleum, designed by Pittsburgh architect Louis Morgenroth in 1862, was the grandest tomb in Allegheny Cemetery for a number of decades. It was originally surrounded by a heavy stone wall, which has long since deteriorated.

For this architectural folly, Morgenroth started with basic Gothic Revival forms (seen in the building's arches and the quatrefoil above the entry), but he also used a number of Classical Revival elements (columns and capitals). Capping his creation, in the words of one architecture critic, is "a dome from outer space."

The brown sandstone structure was built for Kennedy Moorhead, one of the founders of Allegheny Cemetery. Moorhead was a Pennsylvania Canal operator and engineer, and president of the Monongahela Navigation Company, which canalized the Mononga- hela River. The Moorhead mausoleum's crypts are underground; the surrounding family plot is peppered with the graves of generations of Moorheads.

HUCK MAUSOLEUM

Graceland Cemetery
Chicago, Illinois

Perhaps it is fitting that the name of the architect who designed the Huck mausoleum has been lost to the ages, because the building manages to look like an alien space vessel from a *Star Wars* movie. Then again, Chicago has a long tradition of creative and innovative architecture, so what better place to try some experimentation than a cemetery, where few critics ever venture?

Cemetery records indicate the Huck mausoleum was built in 1915, probably by the wife of Louis Carl Huck on a plot Huck purchased in 1888. Besides Mr. and Mrs. Huck, the mausoleum contains the remains of three infants, moved here from other locations. Huck owned the Sheridan apartment building at the corner of LaSalle and Carl Streets in Chicago.

BLOCHER MONUMENT EXTERIOR

Forest Lawn Cemetery
Buffalo, New York

(*Below*) John Blocher designed the exterior of his monument in what must have been some sort of personal vision, since it does not seem to derive from any particular style of architecture. The firm of John McDonnell cut the granite to Blocher's specifications from quarries in Quincy, Massachusetts. The bell, which caps the structure, was cut from a single block. Blocher insisted that it should have no vertical joints. It measures 12 feet in diameter by 12 feet high and weighs 29 tons. The cylindrical stone supports were set upon the foundation. The 29-ton bell was then maneuvered into position and gently lowered into place. Unfortunately, as the capstone was being lowered into place, the rigging timbers gave way and the capstone came crashing down and cracked the bell. A battle in the courts ensued that was actively followed by the local papers. Eventually, the contractor was found liable and another bell was manufactured and put in place without incident.

BLOCHER MONUMENT INTERIOR

Forest Lawn Cemetery
Buffalo, New York

(*Opposite*) Poor Nelson Blocher (1847–84), the man resting peacefully on his back in the diorama inside the Blocher monument/mausoleum (crypts underground). The story goes that he died of a broken heart at age thirty-seven, when he returned from a year abroad to find his beloved Katherine gone. Katherine was a twenty-year-old maid employed by Nelson's father, John Blocher, the Buffalo shoe maven and philanthropist (standing next to his son's body and across from his wife, Elizabeth). Apparently Dad didn't approve of his son's choice of a mate, Katherine being of common stock and Nelson being the son of a great philanthropist. So Dad fired Katherine without telling his son, and when Nelson returned from abroad, Katherine was gone. Nelson searched for her in vain and, so the legend goes, died a year later of a broken heart.

John Blocher, perhaps motivated by guilt, decided to honor his son with this eccentric memorial. Blocher had taken up sculpting and architectural design as a hobby after his retirement. He designed this structure himself.

For the inside of the monument, Blocher carved a plaster model of his son lying on a couch, then hired Paul Roche, a sculptor from Westerly, Rhode Island, to sculpt the real thing. Unfortunately, Blocher was so displeased with Roche's work that he took an axe to it, chopped it to pieces and sent Roche packing. After settling down, Blocher sent photos, as well as measurements and descriptions of his son, his wife and himself, to Frank Torrey, a sculptor in Italy. Torrey produced the pieces using gleaming white Carrara marble. The pieces were then shipped to Buffalo, installed under the canopy and sealed for all time behind specially designed plate-glass windows.

CANDA MONUMENT
Green-Wood Cemetery
Brooklyn, New York

If this monument looks as if it's not quite finished or is perhaps a little, dare we say, unprofessional, it's because it was designed by a teenage girl, not a trained architect or designer. When she was sixteen, Charlotte Canda (1828–45), whose French parents ran a finishing school in New York City, sketched a design for a memorial for her aunt. Little did young Charlotte know that she was actually sketching a monument for herself.

It was a dark and stormy February night (with a snowstorm to boot), and Charlotte was all aglow from her combined seventeenth birthday and coming-out party. Charlotte and her father gave one of her friends a carriage ride home, but as Charlotte's father was escorting her friend to the door, the horses — perhaps afraid of the storm — bolted and ran. Alas, the carriage door had been left ajar and Charlotte was thrown from the carriage, hit her head on the curb and died soon thereafter.

Charlotte's grieving parents asked sculptor Robert Launitz to use the design Charlotte had conceived for her aunt's grave, adapting it as a suitable memorial to their daughter. The result of the Canda/Launitz collaboration has the look of a Gothic Revival wedding cake. Over a century of exposure to the elements has made the ornaments on the marble monument appear to be melting. In the center of the monument, housed in a structure reminiscent of a "grotto" or "aedicula," Launitz carved a statue of Charlotte in the party dress she wore that fateful night. There are seventeen roses circling her head, and the seventeen motif is repeated in the monument, both in its ornamentation and in its dimensions.

To add a touch of Romeo and Juliet to the Canda saga, her despondent fiancé, Charles Albert Jarrett (1819–47), took his own life two years later. Charlotte had been buried on consecrated ground; because Charles had committed suicide, he could not be buried with his bride-to-be. Charles lies off to the right under a coat of arms.

PRATT TOMB

Forest Lawn Cemetery
Buffalo, New York

This canopy tomb looks like a miniature Gothic cathedral, complete with a towering central spire ringed with menacing gargoyles. All four gables are punctuated with trefoils above the Gothic arches, which rest on Corinthian columns. The four larger-than-life female figures standing away from the monument are classically draped, a nod to Classical Revival.

Samuel Fletcher Pratt (1840–80), to whom the monument is dedicated, is only one of many generations of Pratts whose graves pepper the property, which received its first burial in 1872.

OBELISKS

Laurel Hill Cemetery
Philadelphia, Pennsylvania

Laurel Hill Cemetery is a veritable pincushion of obelisks. To break up the monotony, some of the obelisks are draped, while others have been cut off and sprout urns and statues. Further adding to the vertical competition at Laurel Hill is a host of columns, with a variety of objects perched on top.

Obelisks, which are representative of rays of sunlight, were first seen in Egypt during the time of the Old Kingdom. The earliest excavation of an obelisk, dating to the twenty-fifth century B.C. is at Abu Ghurob. It was a massive, fairly squat pyramidal structure set upon a high plinth and was the focal point of the sun temple. During the time of the Middle Kingdom, obelisks made of single slabs of Aswan granite became much taller and slimmer. They were typically erected in pairs in front of selected temples as part of the celebration of royal jubilees. The sides of the obelisk were often inscribed, and its pyramidal top was sheathed in gold to radiate the light of the sun.

WEBB MAUSOLEUM
Woodlawn Cemetery
Bronx, New York

The Webb mausoleum is a structure that defies coherent explanation. Viewing the bottom half, one could make a good case for Classical Revival. Its doubled Corinthian columns, the carvings above the door and the door itself could have come straight from a Roman temple. But from the column capitals upward, the mausoleum begins to look different, like some sort of exotic confection, rather than architecture.

The odd-looking dome, which seems to be melting and dripping over the edges, can be found on a number of mausoleums throughout the country. Perhaps one of the mausoleum builders had a particularly zealous salesman adept at convincing clients to purchase this dome as an out-of-the-ordinary statement. It's not hard to imagine this mausoleum appearing in the pages of *Alice in Wonderland* — all it needs is a rabbit with a watch and a Cheshire cat.

William Webb (1816–99) was a master shipbuilder, whose clipper ships set speed records that still stand. So swift were his ships that one advertisement proclaimed, "Flying Craft for San Francisco, Now Up." In 1853 he launched his last clipper ship, *Young America,* his personal favorite, saying to the mate, "Take good care of her, mister, because after she's gone there will be no more like her." She later set a Liverpool to San Francisco speed record for sail. Fittingly, she did not end her life as a broken-down vessel, sold for scrap; instead, *Young America* was lost at sea in 1886. Webb was realistic and saw steam and steel replacing sail and wood. To that end, he used a considerable amount of his fortune to endow the Institute of Naval Architecture.

LACOSST MONUMENT

Metairie Cemetery
New Orleans, Louisiana

Eugene Lacosst spared no expense when it came to building his final resting place (his will provided $60,000 for his tomb). Built in 1918, during World War I, when building materials were in short supply, the monument is as much a testament to Lacosst's wealth as it is to the craft of its stone carvers. Architects Burton and Bendernagel of New Orleans based their design for the Lacosst monument on a memorial honoring a cardinal in the Church of Santa Croce in Florence, Italy. The Renaissance Revival–style monument, in which the sarcophagus is displayed on a pedestal, takes the form of an exedra, a rectangular or semicircular recess with raised seats.

The cream-colored marble was brought from Alabama quarries to monument manufacturer Albert Weiblen's plant, where expert carvers had been brought from Italy to undertake the intricate and delicate work. The giant sarcophagus housing Lacosst's remains was carved from a solid block of marble and is finished front and back. The architects specified that only the finest pieces of Alabama marble were to be used for the monument; their choices were so precise that the discards were sufficient to build fifteen other mausoleums.

Officially, Eugene Lacosst was a hairdresser, but through crafty speculation, he amassed a huge fortune playing the stock market. Among his other talents was virtuoso whistling and he was often invited to participate in musical events held in people's homes, a popular pastime in the late nineteenth century. Further adding to the curiosities of Eugene Lacosst's life is the provision in his will that his monument should have only enough space for the caskets of himself and . . . his mother.

PIZZATI MAUSOLEUM

Metairie Cemetery
New Orleans, Louisiana

The mausoleum of Captain Salvatore Pizzati was manufactured by Charles Orleans from a design of Orleans architect Charles Brune. There is a strong tradition of aboveground burial in New Orleans, so understandably, a number of mausoleum builders offered their services to New Orleaneans. During the golden age of the mausoleum (post–Civil War to the Great Depression), there was lively competition among mausoleum builders to "build the best" and try to outdo one another. It would appear that the Pizzati mausoleum is the result of that competition: It is one of the most ornate and eclectic mausoleums in the country.

Among its ornaments the Pizzati monument is embellished with medieval turrets, Byzantine columns, curved dentils, a statue of Memory, elegantly carved garlands in the frieze area, a blind window, a draped urn and what appears to be a modified Masonic sign.

Captain Salvatore Pizzati was an Italian immigrant who made his fortune as an importer of tropical fruit. Perhaps Salvatore's mausoleum is just the reflection of a whimsical and somewhat eccentric man: The story goes that before he died, Pizzati requested that he be buried with his favorite rocking chair, and apparently the chair was placed in the chamber below his crypt.

ELKS TUMULUS
Greenwood Cemetery
New Orleans, Louisiana

—❧—

(*Below, left*) An ever-watchful bronze elk peeks over the pediment of the tumulus of the Benevolent and Protective Order of the Elks, Number 30. Although there are only eighteen crypts inside the tomb, the bronze doors secure the remains of dozens of fallen Elks, since the crypts are emptied periodically and the bones are neatly piled elsewhere in the tomb. The tomb was designed by prominent New Orleans monument architect Albert Weiblen in 1912. Weiblen warned the engineer responsible for building the tomb that it needed a strengthened foundation since it was right next to a canal, but Weiblen's advice went unheeded. Seventy-five years later, the tomb has a pronounced tilt.

Above the entablature is a clock with its hands frozen at 11 o'clock, a sacred time to all Elks. At any Elks ritual, the following toast is delivered:

> *My Brother, you have heard the tolling of the eleven strokes. This is to impress upon you that the hour of eleven has a tender significance. Wherever an Elk may roam, whatever his lot in life may be, when this hour falls upon the dial of night, the great heart of Elkdom swells and throbs. It is the golden hour of recollection, the homecoming of those who wander, the mystic roll call of those who will come no more. Living or dead, an Elk is never forgotten, never forsaken. Morning and noon may pass him by, the light of day sink heedlessly in the West, but ere the shadows of midnight shall fall, the chimes of memory will be pealing forth the friendly message, "to our absent Brothers."*

ELKS COLUMBARIUM
Mountain View Cemetery
Oakland, California

—❧—

(*Below, right*) It is hard to put a label on this particular style, so we're just going to call it "Naturalistic." This unique columbarium, reminiscent of megalith and tumulus styles of Neolithic times, was built by the Oakland, California, Elks Lodge to house the ashes of departed Elks and their wives. The columbarium, which was once covered with ivy, is constructed of individual rocks cemented together.

The Elks columbarium is also similar to "grottos" sometimes seen in Catholic cemeteries. Such grottos are reputed to be a good place to go for sightings of the Virgin Mary.

A full-size bronze elk tops the mountain and brays skyward, perhaps signaling the gods of the earthly loss and heavenly gain of another member of the fraternal order. Surrounding the columbarium are the graves of other Elks and their wives.

WHAT'S INSIDE?

A View in the Tomb

Aside from cemetery maintenance workers and the odd family member of the deceased, hardly anyone ever gets to view the inside of a private mausoleum. Sometimes a curious passerby can get a peek, but most of the time what's inside remains a mystery. Apart from the obvious — i.e., bodies, and in some cases cremains (cremated remains) — mausoleums often house extraordinary works of art.

Often, tombs exuberantly decorated on the outside are rather plain on the inside. They simply serve as a resting place for the dead. But in some cases the interiors of private mausoleums are every bit as elegant as their exteriors. There are mausoleums with elaborate inlaid mosaic tile murals. Others contain altars that are used for memorial services. Still others offer magnificent displays of stained glass. Some of these stained glass windows were produced by the famed Tiffany Studios of New York. Tiffany windows worth tens of thousands of dollars have often been the target of art thieves. For that reason, cemeteries have requested that we do not disclose their location.

TIFFANY WITH EMBOSSED SIGNATURE

(*Opposite*) The construction techniques employed in this stained glass window of a levitating angel are typical of the American School of Glass, which was founded in the 1870s by, among others, John La Farge and Louis Comfort Tiffany. Both La Farge and Tiffany were trained as painters and colorists, but saw the booming growth of churches in post–Civil War America as a wonderful opportunity for selling stained glass. The stained glass industry had been steadily declining for over 400 years, and most works that were produced during those four centuries were similar to the transparent paintings-on-glass of Sir Joshua Reynolds.

Members of the American School of Glass advocated the use of opalescent sheet glass, in which variegated colors were blended to form a wide range of tonal effects. They also favored elimination of all painting and staining of window glass except when needed to provide subtle flesh details in the human figure; the use of plating or layering of multiple pieces of glass to achieve depth and delicate color variations; and use of lead lines as an integral part of the design. All of these techniques can be seen in this window.

Tiffany was never at ease designing religious windows. He was not a biblical scholar, nor a particularly adept portrait painter. He relegated most of the work in religious stained glass to a team of designers at Tiffany Studios who were proficient in ecclesiastical window design. Meanwhile, he experimented with different glass techniques and designed secular windows. Tiffany supervised all the production at Tiffany Studios and ensured that all windows were produced in an inimitable Tiffany style.

ANGELS IN FLIGHT STAINED GLASS
Neptune Society Columbarium
San Francisco, California

(*Left*) This "Angels in Flight" stained glass window has been attributed to John La Farge. The use of glass in high relief in the angels' clothing gives the window a three-dimensional quality.

PASTORAL SCENE PAINTED STAINED GLASS

(*Right*) This painted stained glass window bears the inscription "A. L. Brink 165 East 88th Street N.Y., N.Y." Works of art such as this beautiful window have, unfortunately, become targets for thieves, who sell them to unscrupulous art dealers.

One East Coast cemetery has had over 200 stained glass windows stolen. Another cemetery had a 6-foot-by-6-foot Tiffany stained glass window stolen. Replacing that Tiffany window with a modern stained glass window cost over $250,000. Cemeteries have frequently been targets of art theft because they contain a wealth of fine art and have relatively low security. Other frequently stolen items include statues, busts, urns and even tombstones. To combat these thefts, many cemeteries have increased their security in recent years.

MARTIN MAUSOLEUM INTERIOR

Mausoleums were often a showcase for craftspeople and artists. The Martin mausoleum is a masterpiece of Byzantine Revival mosaic tile. A stained glass window completes the impression.

Beautiful stained glass windows adorning many mausoleums are frequently targets of art thieves. Ironically, one of the reasons for building mausoleums was to thwart thieves of a different variety—the "resurrectionists." During the eighteenth and nineteenth centuries, there was a brisk trade in fresh bodies for students to dissect in medical schools. Where better to get a fresh body than from a newly dug grave in a cemetery? Under cover of darkness, "resurrectionists" could easily dig up the loose dirt of a fresh grave, transport the corpse to a waiting doctor and receive a tidy sum for a few hours work. Mausoleums, unlike graves, could be locked, thereby putting one more barrier between the dear departed and the student's scalpel.

GARDEN WALK STAINED GLASS WINDOW

(*Left*) The garden walkway represents the deceased's pathway to heaven. The plantings and pergola serve to enhance and ameliorate the journey.

In the center of this stained glass window is a pergola, a semicovered structure in a garden walkway composed of posts or pillars and surmounted by joists. The pergola frequently became covered by varieties of creeping plants. Although pergolas were but one of a variety of garden elements used by the Victorians, the pergola achieved its greatest popularity in the early twentieth century, with the emergence of the Arts and Crafts Movement.

LILIES AND CYPRESS STAINED GLASS

(*Opposite*) The pastoral scene depicted in this stained glass window features a number of plants often associated with funerary arts. White lilies are a symbol of purity. Originally, in Christian symbolism, the lily was an attribute of virgin saints. Small blue morning glories open to the sun (good) and close to darkness (evil). The evergreen myrtle is a symbol from the Roman mythology of love and was therefore considered sacred to Venus, goddess of love. Cypress trees, with their dark foliage, have since Neolithic times been associated with death because, once cut down, they never spring up again from their roots. Another, more optimistic interpretation is that the tall, narrow shape of the cypress is symbolic of a finger pointing heavenward.

FRENCH GOTHIC INTERIOR

Charles Conick designed the stained glass windows of this French Gothic mausoleum. Great height is achieved in the beautifully crafted sandstone interior by the use of rib vaults supported on engaged columns. The concept of rib vaulting gained great popularity during the twelfth and thirteenth centuries. Fine examples can be seen in the magnificent French cathedrals built during that time.

DEXTER MAUSOLEUM INTERIOR
Spring Grove Cemetery
Cincinnati, Ohio

(*Right*) Below the chapel area of the Dexter mausoleum are the crypts, looking exactly the way crypts are supposed to look. Like the rest of the Dexter mausoleum, these crypts are made of sandstone. Sandstone, especially if it is installed at a certain angle, tends to "melt" over time. The crypts in the Dexter mausoleum are certainly "melting." The rear of the crypt area is illuminated by a shaft which reaches to the upper level chapel behind the altar. This shaft space was intended to contain an elevator for lowering caskets into the crypts, but the elevator was never installed.

CLASSICAL REVIVAL INTERIOR

(*Below*) Elegant white marble floor, ceiling and walls surround visitors in this Classical Revival mausoleum. The mausoleum has eighteen crypts, lots of shelf space for urns and seating for those who wish to linger. The centerpiece of the mausoleum, adding a splash of color, is a stained glass window depicting the Three Fates.

DOGS AND HORSES STAINED GLASS

This pastoral scene decorates the last resting place of a physician who treasured his hands so much that he wore silk gloves all year round, turned door knobs by placing his hand in a coat pocket, and preferred bowing to shaking hands. The stained glass, signed A. L. Brink, New York, depicts what could easily be a summer's day in the English countryside — England being known as a country that encourages and celebrates eccentric behavior.

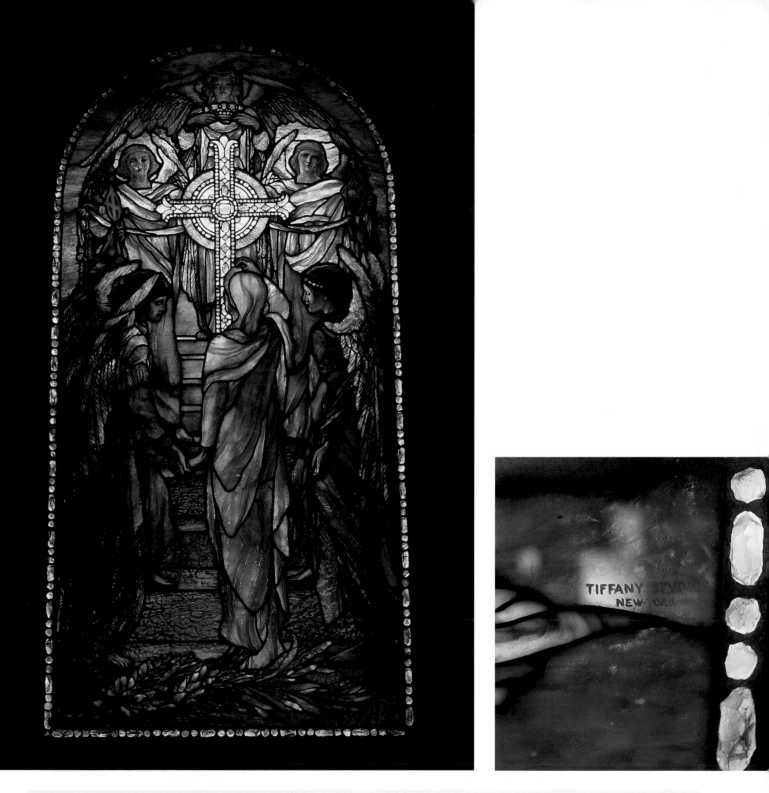

TIFFANY WITH ETCHED SIGNATURE
❧

(*Above, left*) This stained glass window, manufactured by Tiffany Studios sometime after 1900, depicts Mary being crowned Queen of Heaven. Under her feet is a sprig of laurel. Laurel has long been a symbol of triumph, eternity and chastity. In ancient contests, the victor was crowned with it (triumph); laurel leaves never wilt, but preserve their foliage (eternity); and in pagan symbolism, the laurel was consecrated to the Vestal Virgins (chastity).

ETCHED TIFFANY SIGNATURE
❧

(*Above, right*) "Tiffany Studios, New York" was etched into a stained glass window. Tiffany started signing his stained glass after 1890. This particular type of signature appeared after 1900.

ANGELS AND MORTALS
The Human Form in the Cemetery

Although statues are not strictly architecture, they are often used to complement and enhance architecture. The inclusion of statuary as an integral part of an architectural scheme is more apparent in the cemetery. Even a Memorial Day weekend at a cemetery often finds more "humans" frozen in stone than are walking around.

Rural and garden cemeteries provided open space for city dwellers to escape the crowded, noisy and dirty city. The bucolic atmosphere of a parklike cemetery was conducive to creating a public, outdoor sculpture garden. At the time most of the grand cemeteries were established, there were few, if any, public parks and museums.

Cemetery planners, such as landscape architect Frederick Law Olmsted, who designed Mountain View Cemetery in Oakland, California, not only saw their mission as tending to the dead in a tasteful yet efficient manner, they also believed it was their duty to blend art and nature skillfully so as to enhance each for the enjoyment of all. John Jay Smith, one of the designers of Laurel Hill Cemetery in Philadelphia, specifically stated that he wanted to create an outdoor sculpture gallery.

The parade of men, women and angels to be found in cemeteries will please your eyes, gladden your heart and may even bring a smile to your face.

ANDERSEN ANGEL

Cypress Lawn Memorial Park
Colma, California

(*Opposite*) Angels, quite understandably, are the most common form of statuary found in cemeteries. They are meant to represent celestial guides and heavenly companions to the dear departed, while comforting the living and softening the finality of death.

This delicately carved marble angel gazes down in sorrow at the wilted bloom in its hand, signifying the passing souls of Frederik Andersen (1865–1906) and Christine Andersen (1864–1944), both natives of Denmark.

CROCKER ANGEL
Mountain View Cemetery
Oakland, California

This magnificent example of the stone carver's art is one of three unique angels in Mountain View Cemetery in Oakland, California. The seated angel gazing pensively toward the heavens is a common theme in funerary sculpture. In this example, carved in granite rather than marble, the sculptor seems to have captured a very special human quality. The angel is seated on the edge of Mary Crocker's sarcophagus. Mary was the niece of Charles Crocker, one of the "Big Four" of railroading and mining fame.

Glistening in the late afternoon California sun is the obelisk of the Cogswell monument (see pages 88–89).

MARBLE ANGEL
Olivet Memorial Park
Colma, California

On first inspection, this angel appears to be an exact copy of the Crocker Angel in Mountain View Cemetery in Oakland, California, but there are differences. The first difference is obvious: The Mountain View angel is granite and the Olivet angel is marble. The other difference is that, since both of these are hand-carved sculptures, each has a different personality. The marble angel is softer and a bit fuller in the face. The granite angel seems wiser. Maybe it's the eyes, or perhaps the subtle twist of the head or the sculptor's personal style — whatever the case may be, when objects are made by hand, each piece takes on a special character all its own.

MERELLO/VOLTA MONUMENT

Green-Wood Cemetery
Brooklyn, New York

This 8-foot tall bronze sculpture is a depiction of a grief-stricken young woman in her wedding dress. She is clutching a bouquet of flowers and appears to have fallen on the church's steps. Time and weather have only served to make this sculpture more forlorn by etching stains running down her face that look remarkably like tears. Above her, not visible in the photograph, is a rough-hewn cross and the name Merello/Volta. Amazingly, nothing else is known about the monument, but the rumor persists that it commemorates a relative of a gangster shot out of revenge.

STEJSKAL–BUCHAL MAUSOLEUM

Bohemian National Cemetery
Chicago, Illinois

The hooded figure inching toward the Classical Revival Stejskal-Buchal mausoleum, in Chicago's Bohemian National Cemetery, may look like the Grim Reaper but is actually *The Pilgrim*, a bronze statue created in 1929 by the great Czech sculptor Albin Polacek (1879–1965).

Not all Polacek's creations are gloomy. In fact, another of his works in the Bohemian National Cemetery is a partially clad Adonis-like figure, his extended hand reaching for a mausoleum's ringed door handle.

Mr. Stejskal (pronounced "Stay-Skal"), a Czech-American who will spend eternity waiting for the pilgrim to arrive at his door, was a founder of the Novak & Stejskal Bank at the corner of Loomis and Blue Avenues in Chicago.

WARNER MONUMENT

Laurel Hill Cemetery
Philadelphia, Pennsylvania

~~~

The Warner monument, centerpiece of the Warner plot in Philadelphia's Laurel Hill Cemetery, is one of the most curious pieces of funerary sculpture in the United States. It was carved by Alexander Milne Calder, who created the statue of William Penn that stands on top of Philadelphia's City Hall. Calder carved a depiction of a slightly larger-than-life female lifting the lid from the coffin of William Warner (1780–1855) so his soul could be released to the heavens. It is not known if the face of this soul is that of Mr. Warner, or just Alexander Calder's artistic vision. The Calder family is well represented in the arts: Alexander Calder's grandson, also named Alexander, achieved international fame for his mobile and stabile constructions.

Laurel Hill Cemetery, the second oldest garden cemetery in America after Mount Auburn in Cambridge, was established in 1835 on 95 acres of land on a bluff overlooking the Schuylkill River. The Laurel Hill Cemetery Company envisioned a great public park where visitors could view beautiful works of art while strolling through a picturesque landscape. To that end, they employed local architect John Notman. Notman based his plan on the English garden tradition, relying heavily on Kensal Green Cemetery in London for inspiration. Philadelphians flocked to buy plots at Laurel Hill, and it became a popular recreation area and tourist attraction. Indeed, although few visitors come today, it once attracted over 30,000 strollers and art lovers every year.

LARKIN ANGEL

Cypress Lawn Memorial Park
Colma, California

This finely detailed and meticulously carved angel is the work of German-born sculptor Rupert Schmid (1864–1932). Schmid achieved fame as the creator of the Memorial Arch at Stanford University in Palo Alto, California. He was also a director of the San Francisco Art Association and a sculpture instructor at the Mark Hopkins Institute of Art. For Thomas Larkin's memorial at Cypress Lawn, Schmid sculpted an angel holding a feathered pen in one hand and a blank slate in the other. The angel is gazing at a cameo of Mr. Larkin. Larkin's memorial was constructed some time after his death and originally rested above

his grave in San Francisco's vast Laurel Hill Cemetery complex. When San Francisco banished cemeteries from the city in the early twentieth century, Larkin's remains and his angel were moved to Cypress Lawn in Colma.

Thomas Oliver Larkin (1802–58) was the United States' first and last consul to California under Mexican rule. He was a prosperous merchant and an early California pioneer. Together with Mariano Guadalupe Vallejo, he founded the town of Benicia, California, which was California's first state capital. Larkin also introduced the style of architecture that is considered indigenous to California. It consists of a two-story, hipped-roof building with wide, overhanging second-story balconies and is known as the Monterey Colonial Style.

PORTER ANGEL

Allegheny Cemetery
Pittsburgh, Pennsylvania

This huge bronze angel is a replica of a granite angel that once stood in the same place. The Porter monument was built c. 1897. The original granite angel, lingering on the stairs, fell into disrepair. Cemetery records indicate that sometime after 1910 sculptor Brenda Putnam was commissioned to cast in bronze a replica of the angel.

A number of Porters are sheltered in subterranean homes beneath the angel's comforting wings. The best-known resident is Henry Kirk Porter (d. 1921), a builder of light locomotives and a corporator of Allegheny Cemetery.

BIGELOW CHAPEL INTERIOR

Mount Auburn Cemetery
Cambridge, Massachusetts

(*Left*) The ribbed vaults of the Bigelow Chapel's nave reach up to 80 feet in height. The 40-foot-by-60-foot floor area is designed with movable seating so that the chapel can accommodate numbers of different activities. The stained glass windows in back of the altar were manufactured by Ballantyne Allen of Scotland. The uppermost rose window, nestled into the peak of the Gothic arch, is an adaptation of *Night*, a famous relief carving by internationally acclaimed sculptor Bertel Thorwaldsen.

Forward-thinking Bostonians installed a crematory in the basement of the chapel in 1900 and added niches for cremated remains in the East Gallery in 1908.

GREEN-WOOD CHAPEL

Green-Wood Cemetery
Brooklyn, New York

(*Opposite*) Green-Wood Cemetery's magnificent Indiana limestone chapel, built in 1911, is currently being restored. Architects Warren and Wetmore, famous for designing Steinway Hall and Grand Central Station, modeled the Green-Wood Chapel after Tom Tower in the Great Quad at Christchurch College, Oxford.

Tom Tower was designed by famed (some believe the most famous English architect ever) Christopher Wren (1632–1723). Wren received most of his commissions through the Royal Office of Works; however, Tom Tower was an independent commission. Wren was commissioned by John Fell, the dean of Christchurch College, to design the gatehouse building, one of the complex of buildings forming the Great Quad. Wren's adventurous Gothic design included a bulky octagonal tower designed to house a 7-ton bell called "Great Tom." Every evening at 9:05, Great Tom peals 101 times, tolling the original number of students at Christchurch College.

NEPTUNE SOCIETY COLUMBARIUM
San Francisco, California

⟿

(*Above*) Noted architect Bernard J. S. Cahill (1866–1944) designed this magnificent columbarium in 1898. Cahill was especially well known for his designs of funerary architecture. This example is certainly one of his highest achievements, even though he was only thirty-two years old when he received the commis-sion. Cahill's masterpiece is a classic Beaux-Arts design, using elements of baroque, Classical Revival and English Neoclassicism. The columbarium has, in recent years, been given a splash of color by famed San Francisco colorist Bob Buckter, known for his lively treatments of many of San Francisco's elegant Victorian homes. The Neptune Society of Northern California, a division of Sentinel Cremation Society, Inc., operates the columbarium.

NEPTUNE SOCIETY COLUMBARIUM INTERIOR
San Francisco, California

⟿

(*Left*) The three floors of the columbarium contain 4,500 niches for cremains (cremated remains). As of 1997, only about 500 niches were still open. The Neptune Society Columbarium is the only site within the city limits of San Francisco where a civilian's remains may be interred. Today, the military has limit-ed space available for burial of military personnel at the Presidio, which is inside city limits, but is not subject to San Francisco's law banning cemeteries.

LAKESIDE COLUMBARIUM INTERIOR

Cypress Lawn Memorial Park
Colma, California

(*Right*) Even unfinished, the interior of the Lakeside Columbarium is majestic. The finished building was to contain three floors of niches, stained glass, sculpture and meditation areas. Plans are now being considered for its completion.

LAKESIDE COLUMBARIUM

Cypress Lawn Memorial Park
Colma, California

(*Below*) Cypress Lawn's Lakeside Columbarium was designed by San Francisco architect Bernard J. S. Cahill (1866–1944) in 1927. Cahill specialized in mausoleum design and mortuary architecture and was responsible for many of the structures at Cypress Lawn.

The Lakeside Columbarium was one of Cahill's last great creations. He drew his inspiration from the palace of the Roman emperor Diocletian, located in the port city of Spaleto (modern Split) in Croatia. With 10,000 niches, Cahill's columbarium was to be the largest building of its type in the world. Unfortunately, the onset of the Great Depression halted work, and only part of the interior space was finished. With today's rising cremation rates (near 50% in California), the Cypress Lawn board of directors is contemplating completing Cahill's magnificent plan.

QUEEN OF HEAVEN MAUSOLEUM
Chicago, Illinois

Gothic Revival meets the 1950s in this sandstone fortress located 15 miles west of downtown Chicago. The original architectural renderings, drawn in 1954, called for a much sleeker structure and did not include the multicrocketed finials on the tower, but traditional- ists prevailed and the towers and other ornamentation were added. After its construction in 1956, Queen of Heaven became quite popular among Catholics desiring aboveground burial. By 1961 a new section, Queen of Angels, was added; in 1964 came the final stage, Queen of All Saints. The mausoleum triplex contains more than 33,000 crypts, 9,000 of which remain to be filled.

OUR LADY'S CHAPEL

Queen of Heaven Mausoleum
Chicago, Illinois

The Queen of Heaven chapel looks like an ordinary chapel, but look again: Flanking the sides of the chapel are crypts. This style of entombment echoes earlier Christian times when church burial was preferred — the closer to the altar the better the chances of being inched toward heaven by parishioners' prayers. The large stained glass window in back of the altar commemorates the coronation of Mary as Queen of Heaven.

CHAPEL OF THE CHIMES COLUMBARIUM
Oakland, California

(*Above*) California architect Julia Morgan designed major sections of the Chapel of the Chimes columbarium and crematorium from 1926–30. The building has received a number of renovations and additions from 1911 through 1985. Morgan combined Romanesque forms, seen here in the rounded arch, and Gothic forms, seen in the trefoils, quatrefoils and Gothic arches embellishing the windows. To cap her creation, she added a red-tile roof reminiscent of California Mission style. Much of the building is constructed of cast concrete, but the use of Gothic tracery, medallions, sumptuous decorations and massing of spaces gives the Chapel of the Chimes an exuberant and lively quality.

A native of San Francisco, Julia Morgan was the first woman to earn a certificate of architecture from the celebrated École des Beaux-Arts in Paris. She returned to California in 1902 and became a member of an informal "old girls'" network linking the leaders of increasingly active women's organizations. She designed over 700 structures, but her most enduring legacy is her 30-year collaboration with William Randolph Hearst. The best-known Hearst commission was the extravagant "Hearst Castle" at San Simeon, California.

CHAPEL OF THE CHIMES COLUMBARIUM INTERIOR
Oakland, California

(*Opposite*) Cast concrete Gothic arches frame the Frances Willard atrium in the Chapel of the Chimes. Frances Willard was an early leader of women's rights and was the first woman to publicly endorse cremation. Flanking the atrium are small rooms known as chapels. Each chapel entry is decorated with a bronze plaque with an inspirational quotation. The stained glass ceiling was designed and constructed by Marian Simpson of Berkeley, California.

BIRGE MEMORIAL

Forest Lawn Cemetery
Buffalo, New York

Twelve Doric columns stand at attention around the sarcophagus of George K. Birge. The memorial, erected in 1929 by McDonald and Sons of Buffalo, is a good example of the trend in the 1920s and 1930s toward less surface ornamentation.

Rings of columns surrounding buildings are known as peristyles. When the columns are arranged in a circle, as seen here, they are known as tholos forms. The tholos style of architecture is well adapted to constructing buildings of simple, dignified, even ethereal beauty.

George K. Birge, housed in the gleaming white sarcophagus, was a wallpaper manufacturer and president of the Pierce-Arrow Motor Car Company.

SPLANE MAUSOLEUM

Allegheny Cemetery
Pittsburgh, Pennsylvania

The Splane mausoleum, built in 1952 for William W. Splane, a manufacturer of railroad cars, is a splendid example of Modern Classicism. Hallmarks of Modern Classicism, as seen in the Splane mausoleum, are an absence of surface ornament and clean, restrained lines. A pair of engaged columns are the only suggestion of classical form. A realistically sculpted floral panel crowns the entry, while a frieze of debossed panels in an astronomical motif circles the tomb. The placement of the mausoleum's roof was an engineering marvel. The design, using a single slab of granite for the roof, did not allow for use of ropes or hooks during placement. The dilemma was solved by resting the slab on blocks of ice; when the ice slowly melted, the slab slid into place.

TSO MAUSOLEUM

Cypress Lawn Memorial Park
Colma, California

Two marble dog-lions, or shih tzus of Fo, guard the Buddhist mausoleum of Paul Yung Tso. These mythological animals, special guardians of Lord Buddha, teach patience and the subjugation of the ego and its passions. The male, seen here with a ball under its paw, is always located on the east side. The ball is hollow, a symbol of the "emptiness" of the mind in Buddhist spiritual belief. The female dog lion, seated out of view and on the west side, has a baby under her paw. These paired creatures also represent the opposing forces of yin (female) and yang (male). The dog-lions, the other statuary flanking the mausoleum and the positioning of all the elements are part of the *feng shui* of the site. *Feng shui* is an art based on the belief that a harmonious relationship between our environment and nature's forces affects our disposition and fortune.

GERRARD MAUSOLEUM

Spring Grove Cemetery
Cincinnati, Ohio

(*Above*) Built in 1936 for the Gerrard family, this was one of the last of the grand mausoleums built at Spring Grove. Its architecture is entirely appropriate to the times — a blend of Modern Classicism and Art Deco. Its smooth surfaces and restrained embellishments are often seen in public buildings built around the same time. The bronze door is graced by a cutout of a grape tree, reminiscent of the Arts and Crafts style, while the window grills are more Art Deco in their design.

GERRARD MAUSOLEUM DOOR

Spring Grove Cemetery
Cincinnati, Ohio

(*Left*) Although the Gerrard mausoleum is a blend of modern architectural styles, the bronze door, with its grape leaf pattern in the form of a tree, is in the Arts and Crafts style. Arts and Crafts architecture and the corresponding aesthetic flourished in the first few decades of the twentieth century. The style was a reaction to the excessive ornamentation and ostentatiousness of the Victorian era, and proposed a return to simple handmade goods. One of the basic tenets of Arts and Crafts architecture and ornament was the use of natural materials; when that was not possible — as in the case of this bronze door — ornament was sometimes used to express the natural world.

STACHURA MAUSOLEUM

Forest Lawn Cemetery
Buffalo, New York

The Stachura mausoleum, built in 1988, is a modern interpretation of a Greek temple, including a favorite modernist motif — the starburst. Chester and Gloria Stachura designed the bronze bas-relief on the door and had it cast by Rispoli Bronze of Long Island, New York. But the real story here is not about the architecture; it is about love and remembrance.

The plaque above the entry is a representation of two wedding rings with the names Chester and Gloria and their wedding date, July 14, 1956. Most mausoleums are inscribed either with the date of construc-

tion or with the birth and death dates of their occupants; the wedding date on the Stachura mausoleum is unique.

After Gloria died in 1989, Chester would spend long hours outside the mausoleum mourning his dear wife. Then, one day, perhaps fatigued by many hours of standing, Chester decided to have their living room furniture replicated in granite, so he could sit in front of their mausoleum in comfort and remember Gloria in their home. He went to the cemetery board and, after some debate, they granted his request. After all, board members finally agreed, one of the principles of Forest Lawn Cemetery was to make the cemetery accessible and comfortable for the living. On many days, visitors to Forest Lawn Cemetery may see Chester sitting on a stone love seat thinking of Gloria.

GETTY MAUSOLEUM
Graceland Cemetery
Chicago, Illinois

(*Right*) According to the Commission on Chicago Historical and Architectural Landmarks, this delicately ornamented little cube, designed in 1890 by Louis Sullivan, marks "the beginning of modern architecture in America." Never mind that the purpose of the building is to house dead bodies. This opinion is certainly a heavy weight for such a small building to bear. Upon closer inspection, it can be seen that Sullivan did indeed invent a new style, based not on Classical architecture, but on his own ideas. Although critics will always debate which architect and what building signaled the beginning of modern architecture, no one disputes that Sullivan was charting new ground in architectural design.

Sullivan's limestone cube combined strong geometric mass with exquisitely sculpted ornament. Although a century of wear has affected some of the finer etchings, the fundamentals of the design remain. Sullivan kept the bottom half of the mausoleum smooth, which serves as a foil for a maze of octagons. Stars, heralding the ubiquitous starburst designs that would appear in the 1950s, are set into each of the octagons. The bands around the door and windows alternate between smooth and ornamented.

Henry Harrison Getty was a partner in the lumber business with Martin Ryerson. Getty knew of Sullivan's work from the design Sullivan created for Ryerson's mausoleum. Getty commissioned Sullivan to design this mausoleum for his wife, Carrie Eliza Getty, who died in 1890. Henry lived until 1919 and is entombed here with Carrie and their only child, Alice, who died in 1946.

GETTY MAUSOLEUM GATE
Graceland Cemetery
Chicago, Illinois

(*Opposite*) The green patina of age only serves to enhance the beauty of these twin bronze gates. Here Sullivan interlaced geometric and floral forms to achieve a balance between the technological and natural worlds.

SULLIVAN TOMBSTONE
Graceland Cemetery
Chicago, Illinois

(*Below, left*) Louis Henri Sullivan (1856–1924) was one of America's finest architects. His meteoric rise in the often staid profession of architecture is the stuff of legend. By the age of twenty-four he had become a full partner with Dankmar Adler, a noted Chicago architect. Combining Sullivan's gift for designing exquisite ornamentation and Adler's engineering genius, they designed a Chicago landmark, the Auditorium.

Sullivan became a leader in the "Chicago School," which advocated architecture that responded to technology and human needs of the day rather than to past precedents. His bubble burst when the planners of the 1893 Columbian Exposition rejected the innovations of Sullivan's Chicago School in favor of Beaux-Arts classicism. Almost overnight, Sullivan found himself out of work and soon forgotten.

Five years after Sullivan's death, architect Thomas Tallmadge collected funds for Sullivan's granite tombstone. The sculpted sides of the stone represent the development of the skyscraper, and recessed into the stone is Sullivan's profile set against one of his designs.

TSE MONUMENT/MAUSOLEUM

Rosedale Cemetery
Linden, New Jersey

Next to the Tse mausoleum in Linden (a suburb of Newark), New Jersey, stands the monument to young Raymond Tse. Raymond, a sixteen-year-old Chinese-American boy, longed for a Mercedes when he grew up. Unfortunately, he died unexpectedly of pneumonia in 1983, while in Hong Kong as a foreign exchange student.

His family chose to give him the car of his dreams posthumously by commissioning Michael DiPiazza, a monument dealer in Hackensack, N.J., to produce an exact replica of a Mercedes 240D stretch limousine. DiPiazza subcontracted the work to Rock of Ages Granite in East Barre, Vermont. Rock of Ages called

upon two of its best sculptors, Dante Rossi and Warren Sheldon, to produce this stunning work. Rossi and Sheldon carved the monument out of a 34-ton block of granite, using an actual Mercedes as a model. They were further assisted by blueprints supplied by Mercedes Benz.

"They had the car right in front of them," recalls Scott Rahenfuher of Rosedale Cemetery. "What they produced is an exact replica, from the headlights to the grill work, the tail pipes and the windshield wipers. Even the license plate screws are there." It was decided not to sculpt the hood ornament or sideview mirrors, as it was thought they would be vandalized or stolen. "The story goes," says Rahenfurer, "that the boy wanted a Mercedes when he reached driving age, and his older brother promised he'd have one."

The cost of Raymond Tse's Mercedes: $250,000.

TOMB TERMS

altar tomb An aboveground tomb consisting of a sarcophagus mounted on a pedestal.

canopy tomb A large open-air covered tomb supported by pillars or posts. In the center of the canopy is a sarcophagus or other monument.

catacombs Usually, an underground cemetery with tunnels and hallways lined with recesses for caskets and small tombs. Some cemeteries refer to their aboveground community mausoleums as catacombs.

catafalque In architecture, an elaborate tomb consisting of a sarcophagus surrounded by a structure depicting scenes of the deceased's life. In the funerary trade, a raised structure, usually draped, used for displaying a casket.

caveau A chamber underneath a tomb, where bones are swept when room is needed for another body.

cenotaph A memorial or monument to someone who is buried elsewhere.

columbarium A building containing niches for the display or storage of cremains.

cremains Cremated remains.

crypt A chamber for storing bodies.

dromos The passageway into a subterranean tomb or tumulus.

exedra A tomb or memorial with built-in seating.

heroon A mausoleum built to honor a great person or king who has achieved godlike status through his earthly deeds.

house tomb A small tomb, usually made of stuccoed brick, consisting of top and bottom front-loading crypts. The design of most house tombs also includes a caveau underneath the tomb.

hypogeum In antiquity, an underground tomb used by one family or sect.

loculi Side-loaded crypts or holes in walls for bodies.

martyrium A tomb for martyrs.

mastaba An early Egyptian squat, rectangular tomb with slightly tapering sides.

mausoleum A large, imposing tomb, containing crypts and entered through a doorway.

megalith A stone of great size used in the construction of megalithic structures, such as Stonehenge.

obelisk A tall, narrow four-sided monument with a pyramidal top. In Egyptian architecture, it is representative of a ray of sunlight.

ouroboros A circular symbol of a snake eating its tail, signifying immortality.

processional way A roadway used for ritual processions.

receiving vault A building used for storing bodies until their burial space is ready. Often used while a mausoleum is being constructed, or in cold climates, while waiting for the ground to thaw sufficiently to permit grave digging.

sarcophagus A stone coffin used for aboveground burial. In ancient times, limestone was used because it possessed properties that made it quickly dissolve flesh (from the Greek *sarco* + *phagos*, flesh eater).

stele An upright stone slab, surface or pillar bearing an inscription. In ancient Rome, a burial stone.

tumulus An earth-covered tomb projecting above the level of the ground.

vault An underground tomb or a tomb tunneled into the side of a hill. Also, a mausoleum whose architecture is contained in the facade, the sides and back being devoid of ornamentation.

wall vaults Rows of single brick vaults three or four layers high, often seen forming the boundary walls of cemeteries in New Orleans. Also known as side vaults and oven vaults.

BIBLIOGRAPHY

A review of *The Architecture of Death,* by R. A. Eltin. *American Cemetery,* March 1986.

Bergman, Edward F. *Woodlawn Remembers: Cemetery of American History,* Utica, N.Y.: North Country Books, 1988.

Blade, Timothy T. "Highgate Cemetery: London's 'Urban' Burial Ground." *American Cemetery* (March 1990).

Cemetery of Spring Grove: Its Charter, Rules and Regulations, Cincinnati, Oh.: Cincinnati Gazette Office, Wright, Fisher and Co., 1849.

Christovich, Mary Louise, ed. *The Cemeteries,* vol. 3 of *New Orleans Architecture.* Gretna, La.: Pelican Publishing Co., 1989.

Colvin, Howard Montagu. *Architecture and the Afterlife.* New Haven, Ct.: Yale University Press, 1991.

Cronin, Xavier A. "The Cemetery in America." *American Cemetery* (January, April, July, December 1993).

———. *Grave Exodus: Tending to Our Dead in the 21st Century.* New York: Barricade Books, 1996.

Culbertson, Jodi, and Tom Randall. *Permanent New Yorkers.* Chelsea, Vt.: Chelsea Green Publishing Company, 1987.

———. *Permanent Californians.* Chelsea, Vt.: Chelsea Green Publishing Company, 1989.

Curl, James Stevens. *A Celebration of Death.* London: B.T. Batsford Ltd., 1993.

Description de l'Égypte. Paris: Imprimerie Impériale, 1809–1828.

Ferguson, George. *Signs and Symbols in Christian Art.* London: Oxford University Press, 1954.

Fontana, David. *The Secret Language of Symbols.* San Francisco, Ca.: Chronicle Books, 1993.

Gandolfo, Henri A. *Metairie Cemetery, An Historical Memoir.* New Orleans, La.: Stewart Enterprises, 1981.

Harkness, Rosa and Stewart B., Jr. *A History of West Laurel Hill Cemetery.* Bala Cynwyd, Pa., n.d.

Hellman, Peter. "Where History Is at Rest." *New York Times,* September 6, 1996, page C-1.

Howard, Jerry. "The Garden of Earthly Remains." *Horticulture, The Magazine of American Gardening* (September 1987).

Iserson, Kenneth V. *Death to Dust: What Happens to Dead Bodies?* Tucson, Az.: Galen Press, 1994.

Kates, Charles O. "Père Lachaise." *American Cemetery* (June 1984).

Kidney, Walter C. *Allegheny Cemetery: A Romantic Landscape in Pittsburgh.* Pittsburgh, Pa.: Pittsburgh History & Landmarks Foundation, 1990.

Lanctot, Barbara. *A Walk Through Graceland Cemetery.* Chicago, Il.: Chicago Architecture Foundation, 1992.

Linden-Ward, Blanche. *Putting the Past in Place: The Making of Mount Auburn Cemetery.* An offprint from Cambridge Historical Society Proceedings for 1976–1979, pages 171–192.

———. *Spring Grove: Celebrating 150 Years.* Cincinnati, Oh: Cincinnati Historical Society, 1995.

McDowell, Peggy and Richard E. Meyer. *The Revival Styles in American Memorial Art.* Bowling Green, Oh: Bowling Green State University Popular Press, 1994.

Mount Auburn Cemetery archives: Fall 1992 newsletter.

Queen of Heaven Mausoleum. A booklet published by the Archdiocese of Chicago, 1954.

Ragon, Michel. *The Space of Death.* Charlottesville, Va.: University of Virginia Press, 1981.

Reisem, Richard O. and Frank A. Gillespie. *Mount Hope: America's First Victorian Cemetery.* Rochester, N.Y.: Gillespie/Reisem, 1994.

Rotundo, Barbara "Mount Auburn Cemetery: A Proper Boston Institution." *Harvard Library Bulletin,* vol. 22, no. 3 (July 1974).

Sessions, Gene, ed. *Celebrating A Century of Granite Art.* A booklet published for an exhibit at T.W. Wood Art Gallery at the Vermont College Arts Center & Barre Museum by Aldrich Public Library, 1989.

Sloane, David Charles. *The Last Great Necessity: Cemeteries in American History.* Baltimore, Md.: Johns Hopkins University Press, 1995.

Svanevik, Michael and Shirley Burgett. *City of Souls: San Francisco's Necropolis at Colma.* San Francisco, Ca.: Custom & Limited Editions, 1995.

———. *Pillars of the Past: A Guide to Cypress Lawn Memorial Park.* San Francisco, Ca.: Custom & Limited Editions, 1992.

Thomas, Samuel W. *Cave Hill Cemetery: A Pictorial Guide and Its History.* Louisville, Ky.: Cave Hill Cemetery Company, 1985.

Wilson, Samuel Jr. and Leonard V. Huber. *The St. Louis Cemeteries of New Orleans.* New Orleans, La.: St. Louis Cathedral, 1995.

INDEX

6/00   5   10/99
5/02   5   10/99
3/05   (7) 7/03
10/10 (12) 2/10
12/16 (15) 12/16